# Jesus Said What?

# JESUS SAID WHAT?

Words of Jesus That Changed the World

DONALD BROWN

Copyright © 2021 Donald Brown
*Jesus Said What? Words of Jesus That Changed the World*

All rights reserved. No part of this book may be reproduced
Or used in any manner without the prior written permission of the
copyright owner,
Except for the use of brief quotations in a book review.

To request permissions, contact the publisher at
RevDon@SeedsofRevival.org.

ISBN:

First paperback edition, April 2021.

Book Production:
Marvin D. Cloud
mybestseller Publishing

Printed in the USA.

Rev. Donald F. Brown
1020 6th Ave. SE, #117
Aberdeen, SD 57401

www.SeedsofRevival.org

Scripture quotations taken from The Holy Bible,
New International Version® NIV®
Copyright © 1973 1978 1984 2011 by Biblica, Inc.™
Used by permission. All rights reserved worldwide.

## About Donald Brown

Don joined the US Army in 1970. While serving in the Army, Don completed an Associate of Arts degree followed by a Bachelor of Arts degree in Computer Information Systems with Saint Leo University. He retired after a twenty-year career in the US Army as a musician playing euphonium and trombone in various Army bands. Don then entered the Assemblies of God Theological Seminary in Springfield, Missouri. After finishing his Master's of Divinity degree, he pastored for six years in Ellendale, North Dakota, the last five years of which he also taught as Adjunct Faculty at the Trinity Bible College. He taught for a year in Oakland, California, at the Oakland School of Urban Missions, after which he moved to Layton, Utah, to teach computers at Layton Christian academy for four years. Since then, from 2007 on, he has worked as a network security engineer for various enterprises, specializing in various firewalls from Cisco, Juniper Networks, and Palo Alto Networks. He continues to play euphonium and trombone in church. He has been a credentialed minister with the Assemblies of God since 1978 and is the founder of a teaching/preaching ministry, Seeds of Revival Ministries.

# Dedication

This work is dedicated to Jean, the love of my life and wonderful wife of over 46 years. Her encouragement and belief in me, even when I had none, has been a constant inspiration.

# Acknowledgments

I give thanks to several people for their invaluable guidance, advice, and encouragement. This project began with my idea for teaching an adult elective in a midweek class. Executive Pastor, Rev. Rob George, encouraged me to consider having the sessions recorded so that we could develop the content into a podcast. I taught the weekly class in the Fall of 2019. With the advent of the COVID-19 Pandemic in early 2020, the podcast development from the recordings fell by the wayside. I had the recordings transcribed by the AllTranscriptions.com service. Rev. Marvin D. Cloud assisted greatly with editing the content into the present body of work.

# Table of Contents

Foreword by Dr. G. Robert Cook Jr. — *xiii*

Introduction — 1

Chapter 1: Mary, Jesus' Mother Said What? — 3

Chapter 2: Sermon On the Mount: The Beatitudes — 27

Chapter 3: Sermon On the Mount You Have Heard It Said — 43

Chapter 4: Sermon In the Valley — 69

Chapter 5: I Am, Part One — 97

Chapter 6: I Am, Part Two — 123

Chapter 7: Final Statements — 147

# Foreword

I remember well as a young lad growing up trying to read my New Testament after my Sunday School teacher diligently endeavored to teach me Bible stories and biblical principles. The stories about Jesus always intrigued me, and I seemed drawn to the Gospels, those parts of the New Testament that focused on the life and words of Jesus. The actual Bible I used as a young boy was a King James Version and it was a "red letter edition," meaning that the words attributed to Jesus printed in red. That printing format made it easier for me to concentrate on what Jesus said.

Many times as I read the words of Jesus, and honestly, other parts of the New Testament, I often asked myself, *What does that really mean? That sounds a bit revolutionary; what was He saying?* Over the past 60 plus years since those days as a lad, I have continued to read those same passages, and though I have done extensive study as a learner and teacher, there are still times when I will read a passage and think, *What does that really mean? What was Jesus saying when He said those words?*

My friend, Donald Brown, has tackled in this book the needful assignment of answering some of those questions I used to have as a young boy but often still have as a grown man. The title of the book helps to sum up the author's intent, and we could rephrase it by asking: Can you run that by me again? Did Jesus actually say that? If so, what did He mean? In his conversational style (at times it seems like Don Brown is talking into your ear rather than writing to you), he shares practical help in figuring out what Jesus meant when He talked to the crowds, when He talked to His close followers, His disciples. The Bible will come alive to the reader as the author shares background material, plus needed perspectives that arise from looking at the Greek or Aramaic text from which our English Bible originated.

Fasten your seatbelts, put on your thinking caps (as my Sunday School teachers used to tell me), and allow this poignant treatise to encourage your faith, stretch your knowledge about Jesus and his words, and help you spread to others the good news of Jesus and His eternal message.

**Dr. G. Robert Cook Jr.**

Grand Junction, CO
*Former President of the Alliance for Assemblies of God Higher Education*
*Former District Supt. of the Rocky Mountain District of the Assemblies of God*

# Introduction

This book began with my idea for teaching an adult elective in a midweek class. The title, *Jesus Said What?* captures the approach attempted here. For example, when Jesus said in the Sermon On the Mount, "You have heard that it was said, 'Do not commit adultery.' But I tell you that anyone who looks at a woman lustfully has already committed adultery with her in his heart," His hearers on that mountainside had a "Jesus Said What?" moment.

When the executive pastor asked me if I could record the classes in order to produce a podcast from them, I was excited about the idea. Unfortunately, that was about the time the COVID-19 Pandemic changed everyone's plans in early 2020, the podcast included. I sent the recordings to a transcription service to have them put in written form.

The concept of the book series is to take a closer look at the words of various writers or speakers in the New Testament to see how they profoundly affected the world, both then and through to the twenty-first century. Since the book's content began as a live presentation, I have attempted to maintain that same sense of informal intimacy that the attendees experienced during the live sessions.

During the class presentation, we gave a handout of the actual Scriptures referenced in the session to all participants in order to give them room for taking notes. I presented the material from a notebook computer with the New International Version (NIV) of the Bible displayed on the left half of the screen, and the Greek New Testament displayed on the right half of the screen. In the book, I attempted to assure the quoted Scriptures are the NIV, but sometimes in the transcription process the person or persons that did the work may not have accurately understood what they heard. Also, related to that, a phrase by phrase discussion of the Scriptures ensued, therefore, I sometimes paraphrased or added descriptive language to the presentation in order to illustrate or clarify statements. In addition, since this was a live session, sometimes, chapters may include questions or comments raised by participants.

The goal was to take a serious, but fresh and new approach to the Scriptures being studied. Though the language may seem casual, the words of the text received serious study, and the conclusions drawn from weighty contemplation. The point of this book is that words and language matter, both in the original Greek and in contemporary English. This is a journey back to the times and culture in which Jesus found Himself in order to capture the full depth and breadth of what He said. His words did, after all, change the world.

# CHAPTER 1

# Mary, Jesus' Mother, Said What?

*Father in Jesus' name, we thank You Lord for this time that we have together. We pray Your blessing upon everyone who reads this book. We ask You Lord to speak to our hearts and let your word penetrate our spirit in a powerful way. Let Your Holy Spirit guide our conversation and guide our hearts and our minds as we seek Your word and Your voice in the midst of Your Word. We thank you and praise You in Jesus' name. Amen.*

In *Jesus Said What?* we will talk about some things that Jesus said in the New Testament and see what we can learn from them. It's a fresh approach, I think. It is original content, and here is the process we use. We will look at some passages of Scripture and hear what was said, and look at the original language, where it's appropriate. We will see if we can kind of dig up some good solid stuff, some jewels, out of the ground of Scripture.

To explain a little further concerning the approach taken in *Jesus Said What?* and what it means, I will use the example of Nicodemus in John 3:21. He came to see Jesus in the dark of night and he said, "We know you are from God because only someone from God can do the things that you do." And Jesus said, "Nicodemus, you can only go to heaven by being born from above." Nicodemus had a *Jesus Said What?* moment.

I have noticed in Scripture that Jesus answers the real question, even if it's not the question an individual may ask. Have you ever noticed that in your own lives? I know for me, I will ask Him one thing and He will say something completely different. Then I realize that's the relevant thing I should have been thinking about. Jesus let Nicodemus know the issue was being born again. The issue wasn't to come and pay homage to Him and compliment Him. Jesus didn't even respond to that. There are a lot of those moments throughout the Gospels and we will touch on some of them.

I started life as the son of an atheist father, and my mom was an Episcopalian because that's what she grew up in. I didn't come to Christ officially until many years later as an adult. However, a lady who lived around the block introduced me to Christ when I was about four years old. She was a Sunday school teacher who asked me if I wanted some milk and cookies and then told me about Jesus. I went home and told my dad. Of course, he immediately poo-poohed it and said it was only what some people believe, but it was silly.

As an adult, I ran into some people called Christ Is the Answer. They were a bunch of long-haired saved hippies, part of the so-called Jesus People movement. That's where I met my wife. She was with them. She came up and asked the guy who they tasked with taking me around to introduce us. We married a year later in 1974.

God knows what He is doing, and He often does it far in advance. I went to the Assemblies of God Theological Seminary after retiring from the Army and I received a Master's of Divinity degree. I did a little bit of post-graduate work. But my genuine passion is teaching. I also taught at Bible College level. Hopefully, that will come across in a positive, helpful, and constructive way. I hope you enjoy this material.

There is a lot of stuff in the Word that we don't always have time to get to and to dig out. Our purpose here is not to speed through and come up with a bunch of little cool quotes. Our purpose is to take our time through these passages. But we will hopefully have a good time as we go through this material.

I figure the best place to start is with Mary, the mother of Jesus. Let's see what Mary has to tell us. In Luke 1:26-38 (NIV), we read:

> "In the sixth month, God sent the angel Gabriel to Nazareth, a town in Galilee, to a virgin pledged to be married to a man named Joseph, a descendant of David. The virgin's name was Mary. The angel went to her and said, 'Greetings, you who are highly favored! The Lord is with you.' Mary was greatly troubled at his words and wondered what kind of greeting this might be. But the angel said to her, 'Do not be afraid, Mary, you have found favor with God. You will be with child and give birth to a son, and you are to give him the name Jesus. He will be great and will be called the Son of the Most High. The Lord God will give him the throne of his father David, and he will reign over the house of Jacob forever; his kingdom will never end.' 'How will this be,' Mary asked the angel, 'since I am a virgin?' The angel answered, 'The Holy Spirit will come upon you, and the power of the Most High will overshadow you. So the holy one to be born will be called the Son of God. Even Elizabeth your relative is going to have a child in her old age, and she who was said to be barren is in her sixth month. For nothing is impossible with God.' 'I am the Lord's servant,' Mary answered. 'May it be to me as you have said.' Then the angel left her."

Now the sub-question I ask is, what would you think? Perhaps you know someone who gets sort of weird around celebrities, for example. It might depend on the celebrity, but people often do that. I wouldn't call it stage fright, rather they are star-struck. They might get tongue-tied. Perhaps they can't say anything, or do anything. They aren't sure what to say if they could say anything. Other people sort of take it as they go, and then it works out.

When the angel Gabriel showed up, how did Mary know he was an angel? Probably because he looked different, or maybe he wore shiny clothes. We don't have a description to know that. One of the first things you learn about Bible study is we don't want to jump to conclusions or develop some ideas that we once thought and therefore those ideas must be true every time we see them. An angel does not always have big white feathery wings or a sword. What we know though is, the angel confronted Mary oddly. "Greetings, you who are highly favored, the Lord is with you." Now I would like to hear that. I also want to hear on the last day, "Enter into my Kingdom, good and faithful servant." But she certainly wasn't expecting that.

Most of the time when an angel comes to someone and says something, the angel will start out with something like, "Do not be afraid." Sometimes, people will even fall down as dead, or fall down to worship the angel, in which case the angel might say something like, "Don't worship me, I serve God just like you do." Why did the angel start that way? Why didn't he start with a normal, "Don't be afraid"? We don't know, but he must have had a reason. "Greetings, you who are highly favored" certainly set the stage for an interesting conversation.

Since he brought greetings to a highly favored Mary, it might be helpful to look at that word "favored" and think about what it could mean. Favored could mean a bunch of things. We assume she knew he was an angel. I wonder what went through her head? To the ladies reading this, you have all been thirteen to sixteen years old. That's about the age Mary was when this took place. They didn't have the teen culture that we have now, where everything is all twittery and no one takes anything seriously. Back then, they took everything seriously. They grew up a lot faster, and they prepared for life a lot earlier. And they prepared for the end of life a lot sooner too. The lifespan of people by this time had gone down from hundreds of years to a few decades. Now, it's a little more, but the entire culture of that time was different.

What would a thirteen to sixteen-year-old girl think, when an angel, obviously a creature of different normal description than what she was used to, said to her right out of the blue, "Greetings, you who are highly favored. The Lord is with you"? What might you have thought if that happened to you? Would you have thought he had the wrong address? Would you have felt reassured by what he said? Is it possible you would be ready to hear what he said next because he quieted your fears? Perhaps he addressed whatever emotional condition she was in to allow her to receive his message.

The angel troubled Mary, but she didn't say she was afraid, or anything like that. Normally in the Bible, an angel appears to people and they are a little afraid. Yes, the angel's words troubled Mary, therefore she thought the whole time about what it was. It seems like she was pretty calm. She was pretty composed for someone at that age. I think it's pretty awesome, actually. Perhaps that's partly why God favored her. The Lord knew she would take it pretty well. There is probably something to be said for that.

I think the initial observation that the angel's greeting was unusual is interesting and worth focusing on for a minute. We have talked about this young lady; the virgin named Mary. Mary was greatly troubled at his words and wondered what kind of greeting this might be. But the angel said, "Don't be afraid, Mary, you have found favor with God." If she wasn't already at ease as I suggest, hopefully, he was putting her at ease now. He didn't want the message to get lost in the emotional turmoil that could overwhelm her. Because this message is important to me, I assume it's important to you. This is not something you want to take lightly. When the angel approaches her this way, he troubled her and she wondered what kind of greeting this might be. I wonder what she wondered? Such as, *Am I in trouble? Do I have to go to the principal's office? Is he sure he has the right address, the right place? Am I the right person?* I mean, what kind of greeting might this be? But the angel said to her, "Do not be afraid, Mary, you have found favor with God."

Now, what else do you notice there? "Do not be afraid, Mary." He knew her name. He didn't have to ask, "Are you Mary? Are you sure?" He knew her. Obviously, this guy had something going. The angel said to her, "Don't be afraid, Mary, you have found favor with God. You will be with child and give birth to a Son, and you are to give Him the name, Jesus. He will be great and will be called the Son of the Most High. The Lord God will give him the throne of his father, David, and he will reign over the house of Jacob forever, his Kingdom will never end!"

Let's unpack that a little. There is a lot in there. I don't know that the angel said it in a rush, but it certainly is a lot of information. Having found favor with God, he then tells her, "you will be with child." That was not probably her next plan. Why? Because she was betrothed to Joseph.

Betrothal is a step beyond the engagement of our modern culture. Today, people get engaged and unengaged at the drop of a hat.

"Let's get married."

"Okay."

"I don't want to."

"Okay."

It's a lot less serious for some people. But in Mary's time, a lot of preparation and planning came with being betrothed. There are huge promises, not between the two individuals only, but between the families of the individuals. With betrothal, there is a dowry and all kinds of consideration and preparation.

Do you remember the story of the virgins, some who were wise, and some who were not? (Matthew 25:1-13) The ones who were not wise didn't have enough oil. The ones who were wise had extra. The ones who weren't wise ran into town, but by the time they got back, the wedding procession had passed them by.

We in the West are generally linear thinkers. We carry watches, cell phones, and other devices to keep us on track through our daily lives. Calendars, appointments, events, schedules, and so on, seem to rule our existence. We consider events in terms of when they start and end. We plan when to leave, what time to arrive, how long the event will last, and how long to return home or arrive at the next scheduled event in our day.

In other parts of the world are many cultures where people are concrete thinkers. They understand events in terms of the event as a whole. As an example, in many cultures in Africa, if you get invited to a wedding and the wedding starts on Saturday at 9 a.m., if you show up on Saturday at 9 a.m., ready for a wedding, you would find yourself embarrassed. Because Saturday at 9 a.m. is when all the preliminary preparations begin. If the family is large, they get together as they cook and prepare and make dishes and all kinds of related activities take place on Saturday. But nothing official will happen until all the rest of the more distant relatives arrive, maybe on Monday or Tuesday or whenever they get there. Then and only then do they all gather in one place, and follow the groom to the other end of town to where the feast will take place.

And that's what took place with those virgins. Preparations for the wedding had been ongoing for some time. When the groom's party begins its journey across town to the site of the actual wedding ceremony, people had lined up along the route the entourage would follow. As the groom passed, the expectant crowd would fall in behind as part of the wedding party. When the groom arrived at the destination and passed into the facility followed by the folks who had joined along the way, the gates were then closed behind the last of the group and the festivities could finally begin.

All of this stuff has to be laid out. It's not as simple as you get a preacher, a church, buy a fancy dress, rent a tuxedo, and you show up and have some cake and eat and it's over. A lot of planning takes place. But betrothal is more than an engagement on another level as well, because it requires a divorce to end it. You don't just say one day, "Well, let's not be engaged anymore." It didn't work like that. It's a serious undertaking. She is already being told that she will give birth to a son.

Not only did the angel tell her she would be with child and give birth to a son which is pretty important too, back in that culture, he then added, "you are to give him the name Jesus." Now the name Jesus in Aramaic and Hebrew basically is a derivation of Jehovah Saves, Iēsous. Isaiah 7:14 says, "For a virgin will give birth to a son. And he shall be called Immanuel, God with us." Matthew 1:23 also quotes it. Immanuel, God with us, Jehovah saves, Jesus, Joshua is a variant of that same thing. That is a theme that runs through Hebrew Scriptures. These are salient features of the angel's message to Mary to prepare her for what is ahead.

"You are going to be with child, you are going to give birth to a son and you are to give him the name, Jesus." There are three huge things right there in one sentence. Then the angel says that he will be great and will be called the "Son of the Most High." Now, things are getting quite strange. "The Son of the Most High" gets beyond the realm of mortal humanity. "The Lord God will give him the throne of his father David." In Jewish culture that is huge, because David was the Son of Promise and he was the one who had God's honor, the man after God's heart. David was full of flaws; he killed, he lied, he had adultery with a woman, but he was God's choice. There was a passion in David. And Mary's son would be called the Son of David and would sit on his throne, the throne of David.

"He will reign over the house of Jacob forever, his kingdom will never end." Now we step beyond the human realm for sure because we look out into eternity, and we get a cosmic view of what's going on, way past human history, both in scope and in time. This little thirteen to sixteen-year-old girl hears some pretty heavy stuff right here. But after she hears all this, she didn't appear to bat an eyelash. She says, "How will this be, since I am a virgin?"

Mary's question introduces the next major part. We become aware of the angel's next words as the role of the Holy Spirit in this entire process. Nowhere in the Bible does the word Trinity exist. Did you know that? It's not in the Bible, you can't find it. The doctrine of the Trinity, however, is well-founded in the Bible, and this is one of the linchpin points in the New Testament that we are about to view. But I want to give you a quick tiptoe through the whole thing.

Back in the Garden of Eden, there was a conversation, "Let us make man in our image," and then, "He made him, then man and woman, He created them."

There was another conversation. God met up with Adam and Eve in the Garden and said, "Where are you guys?"

Adam said, "We were hiding in the bushes because we were naked."

"Who told you, you were naked?"

And then shortly after that, after He got the runaround, He looked at Adam because he was the one dumb enough to speak up.

"Well, this woman you gave me."

Guys, never do that! Don't blame it on your wife first, or at least get out of the room before you do, right?

And then the Lord said to Eve, "Well, who told you?"

And she said, "Well, this serpent."

He didn't even ask the serpent, because He knew that's where it started.

Then He said, "And I will put enmity between you and the woman, and between your offspring and hers; he will crush your head, and you will strike his heel" (Genesis 3:15, NIV). The King James version reads, "And I will put enmity between thee and the woman, and between thy seed and her seed; it shall bruise thy head, and thou shalt bruise his heel." Many see this as the first mention of Jesus in the Bible.

Another conversation took place a little later in the garden of Eden. In so many words, God said, "We need to get them out of the garden, lest they partake of the tree of life and become like us and live forever."

This was not a punishment, but a blessing. By explanation, we can ask whether the devil could be saved if he wanted to be? The answer is revealing. While the devil is not likely to request forgiveness of his sin, even if he asked forgiveness, it is unlikely that it is available to him. We find the entire focus of salvation in John 3:16 (NIV), "For God so loved the world that he gave his one and only Son, that whoever believes in him shall not perish but have eternal life." God's plan of salvation was specifically for man, not for the devil and his demons. The devil can never get saved because he cannot die, and therefore nobody can die in his place. Adam and Eve could die. Therefore, God had to get them out of the Garden of Eden before they, like the devil, become unable to die by partaking of the tree of life. If that ever happened, no one could die in their place.

Fast forward to Mary. The Angel Gabriel arrives and says something profound to Mary, who asks, "How will this be since I am a virgin?" The angel answered, "The Holy Spirit will come upon you, and the power of the Most High will overshadow you. So the holy one to be born will be called the Son of God."

Now here is Eve's seed. Mary is the fulfillment of that prophetic statement by God in the Garden. The angel in explaining this to her, tells her, "The Holy Spirit will come upon you, the power of The Most High will overshadow you." That's interesting, all by itself. God is doing an active creative work here in preparing her to receive His only begotten son. The original Greek word in John 3:16 is *"monogenes,"* pronounced mo-no-ge-nays. Mono means "one" or "only" and *genes* means "beginning." *Monogenes* son has a simple translation. "Only Begotten Son," or "One and only Son."

The angel then added that the holy one to be born will be called the Son of God. This is extremely important. This establishes the fact that the Holy Spirit is God. We already know about God in the Garden of Eden. Now the angel is saying the child will be called the Son of God and is referred to in that capacity as the Holy One to be born. We have a rough sketch already right here, of the Triune Godhead. The Father isn't mentioned specifically, but "the Holy Spirit will overshadow, will come upon you and the power of the Most High will overshadow you. So the holy one to be born will be called the Son of God. Even Elizabeth, your relative is going to have a child in her old age. And she who is said to be barren is in her sixth month, for nothing is impossible with God." Wow, this is a tour de force. What an introduction. What a layout for the plan of the ages, right here in this little room, for this angel talks to Mary and she is not batting an eyelash. She was a little concerned, a little troubled, but she asks good, cogent questions. She does not lose a step.

The angel says the Holy Spirit will come upon her and nothing is impossible with God and that stitches together the idea that there is another aspect of God, besides the Father. And now we find the inkling of the idea of the Son of God, and that the Holy Spirit is clearly portrayed as God as well. There is a lot of stuff hanging on these branches, so to speak. Okay, nothing is impossible with God. How does she respond? "I am the Lord's servant. May it be to me as you have said," then the angel left.

Her last statement was then to submit, to acquiesce as to what God wanted from her. Only five minutes before, Mary was minding her own business, a young girl doing normal things in her normal life, getting ready to be married to a pretty cool guy who is a carpenter. He made pretty good money, etc., and things looked pretty good. Suddenly this angel shows up and stirs everything up and then left.

What does she do? Mary got ready and hurried to a town in the hill country of Judaea where she entered Zechariah's home and greeted Elizabeth, her cousin. When she heard Mary's greeting, Elizabeth's baby leaped in her womb, and Elizabeth was filled with what? The Holy Spirit. There is that Holy Spirit again. It's an interesting moment. In a loud voice, Elizabeth exclaimed, "Blessed are you among women, and blessed is the child you will bear! But why am I so favored, that the mother of my Lord should come to me? As soon as the sound of your greeting reached my ears, the baby in my womb leaped for joy. Blessed is she who has believed that what the Lord has said to her will be accomplished!" That's a lot for saying, "Hey, Elizabeth," right?

At the beginning of this conversation, when she arrived, she entered and greeted Elizabeth. We don't know what she said. But there was some reaction that was beyond human and beyond normal because the baby leaped in Elizabeth's womb. Now I don't know if that's the beginning of dancing in the Spirit or not. But I have an idea since the Holy Spirit is again here, in a loud voice, "Blessed are you," Elizabeth receives the Holy Spirit and she prophesied. She spoke information to which she had no natural access.

Do you remember when Saul hung out with the prophets and he started prophesying when they appointed him as the king of the Jews? This happens when you get filled with the Holy Spirit.

We see things like that, later on in the Book of Acts, we see the Holy Spirit come down and people prophesying, glorifying God, etc. The Holy Spirit has a powerful effect and in a loud voice, Elizabeth exclaims and prophesied, "Blessed are you among women, and blessed is the child you will bear." When the angel talked to Mary, Elizabeth was already six months pregnant. Mary went straight away there, she didn't wait. Mary probably didn't show. But Elizabeth supernaturally conveyed the information that this is something powerful. And it confirmed what Mary had already heard from the angel.

If you ever wonder if things you say matter, they do. And these are momentous conversations that take place here. The words people say transform history when they deal with things of God. In a loud voice, she exclaimed, "Why am I so favored that the mother of my Lord should come to me?" She prophetically recognizes and acknowledges this Son, this child, as God, as Lord. "As soon as the sound of your greeting reached my ears, the baby in my womb leaped for joy."

All we are told before that is Mary's greeting, and when Elizabeth heard it the baby leaped, and the Holy Spirit filled Mary. But here, Elizabeth says, "as soon as the sound of your greeting reached my ears, the baby in my womb leaped for joy. Blessed is she, who has believed that what the Lord has said to her will be accomplished." Her assumption was joy, but I imagine that was probably transferred to her as well. These are things that don't normally happen, and Mary then begins a song. We have reused this song many times in different ways. I learned a portion of it, "My soul doth magnify the Lord, and my spirit hath rejoiced in God my Savior, for He that is mighty has done great things, and holy is His name. My soul doth magnify the Lord." That's from the King James Version, more or less. We know this as the Magnificat. I don't know if you ever heard of that. If you have a Catholic background, it's possible you have. Mary says, or sings,

"My soul glorifies the Lord, my spirit rejoices in God my Savior, for He has been mindful of the humble state of His servant. From now on all generations will call me blessed."

I want to talk a little about a couple of words. First, what does humble mean? Does it mean you sort of mope around all day long and never take a compliment? If you ever hear, "You are a pretty good-looking guy," or "You are a pretty good-looking lady," and you respond, "Oh, no, I am not." Is that humble? No. What happens when people acknowledge things that are part of how God has made you, when you disavow them? There is no humility there. That's kind of a slap in God's face, because He made you the way you are and He did it on purpose, believe it or not. She said, "He has been mindful of the humble state of His servant." Notice how she refers to herself in the third person, (His servant), and she says, "He has been mindful of the humble state of His servant. From now on all generations will call me, blessed." This is another word. Blessed, in Greek, implies joy and overflowing happiness. This isn't some religious word that doesn't have much meaning. It has a powerful and positive impact on our lives. Here's a history lesson. If you remember, one of the first things said in the Declaration of Independence is that all men are endowed by their Creator with certain unalienable rights, including life, liberty, and the pursuit of happiness. Happiness comes straight from God. In case you ever get confused by political rhetoric, joy and overflowing happiness still come from God, even if people don't accept the document it's written in, because the original document it is written in, is called the Bible.

And so, "They will call me blessed, for He has performed mighty deeds" or "The mighty one has done great things for me, Holy is His name, His mercy extends to those who fear Him from generation to generation." This is the 13 to 16-year-old girl. She is really digging deep into this stuff. Are you getting this? She's a young teenager. "His mercy extends to those who fear Him from generation to generation. He has performed mighty deeds with His arm. He has scattered those who are proud in their inmost thoughts. He has brought down rulers, scattered them." What does that remind you of?

The Tower of Babel in Genesis 11:1-9. Pretty powerful people wanted to ascend to the heights of the Most High God. He brought them low. And Mary is talking about that. He scattered those who are proud in their inmost thoughts. He has brought down rulers from their thrones but has lifted up the humble. "He has filled the hungry with good things but has sent the rich away empty." That's an interesting comparison. "He has helped his servant Israel, remembering to be merciful to Abraham and his descendants forever. Even as He said to our fathers." Mary stayed with Elizabeth for almost three months and then returned home. That's profound stuff for Mary. She clearly knew her history. I don't know, I can't really say that this is in the same category as prophecy, but it sure feels almost prophetic. It certainly is drawing out some pretty heavy ideas for a little girl, a young lady. We could almost see it as prophetic in the same way Elizabeth spoke. She spoke things she had no other way of knowing. Mary recounts history. It's not necessarily prophetic, but she also connects some pretty hefty thoughts during that moment. I don't think that's by accident. I don't think she was a well-trained, well-groomed theologian, by any means.

My question is, where does that come from? The Holy Spirit. Not everything the Holy Spirit does, and not everything a person says is necessarily prophetic. But Mary said things that wouldn't normally come from the mouth of a person that young.

Now, this next part is interesting. We skip forward to Luke 2:16-19 when the shepherds are told about the birth of Jesus.

> "So they hurried off and found Mary and Joseph, and the baby, who was lying in the manger. When they had seen him, they spread the word concerning what had

been told them about this child, and all who heard it were amazed at what the shepherds said to them. But Mary treasured up all these things and pondered them in her heart."

Again, that's not characteristic of a young teenage girl. I once tried to describe what my wife went through with the birth of our first child in a poem. I did it in Shakespearean sonnet form, which uses iambic pentameter and a structured rhyming pattern. The tagline at the end is, "For childbirth is difficult, you know," which probably understates it, but it is something that men have long been unable to understand.

The Magi had visited Mary, and they showed up with their gifts of gold, incense, and myrrh, but she maintained her presence of mind and "treasured up all these things and pondered them in her heart." That's a pretty wise and measured response to such momentous events. She didn't say anything here in that sense, but what was going on in her heart spoke volumes about what she might have said.

Mary, as it turns out, was an excellent choice. We are talking about God. He is going to make the right choice, right? But she pondered these things; she didn't get all weirded out. Mary tried to understand them instead of leaping to conclusions. She let them take their place in her heart as she continued to observe the unfolding events following her son's birth.

Mary didn't discard these events or their importance, but she also didn't try to over-explain them. When we catch the meanings of treasured and pondered, it's different from jumping to conclusions one way or the other. She took the long view and let things work out.

Let us move forward a little more, to Luke 2:41 where we look at the annual journey made to the oldest and most important religious festival in Judaism. Every year the parents of Jesus went to Jerusalem to the feast of the Passover. I hope you all know the story of the Passover in the background, what's behind it. The Israelites were in Egypt and God delivered them from the Egyptians. After God had visited the plagues upon the Egyptians, the Israelites were to take a first-year lamb that had never been shorn, with no blemishes, and prepare that lamb for a meal. No part of that lamb was to be left. It was all to be eaten; no leftovers. Each family left a seat open at their table down through the centuries in case the prophet Elijah appeared. He would have a seat at the table. That thus instituted the first Passover. Each family would splash the blood from their lamb on the doorway's sides and top so that the Lord would pass over them. "At midnight the LORD struck down all the firstborn in Egypt, from the firstborn of Pharaoh, who sat on the throne, to the firstborn of the prisoner who was in the dungeon, and the firstborn of all the livestock as well" (Exodus 12:29).

The Passover looked forward to something profound, specifically to when Jesus was born from Mary and laid in that manger. By the way, a manger was a feeding trough, and they were not clean. We picture nice pristine shining hay, but cattle and other livestock would go in there and lick and slobber as they ate the hay, their keepers would add more hay on top of the old hay. They would lick, slobber, and eat it, and then they put a baby in it. Hopefully, they didn't lick and slobber on the baby. Now, as a young boy, every year his parents went down for the feast of the Passover in Jerusalem, which is one of the huge memorial events in the history of the Jewish people.

When he was 12 years old, they went up to the feast according to the custom. He is younger than Mary was when she got the news about His birth. After the feast was over, while His parents returned home, the boy Jesus stayed behind in Jerusalem, but they were unaware of it. They thought He was in their company; they traveled on for a day, then they looked for Him among their relatives and friends. Now you may wonder how that can happen? They didn't all bundle into the car, look around, and say, "Okay everybody is here, let's go."

Walking to your destination you stroll along, and friends walk with friends and they knew He might be back there talking to somebody or who knows what. It would be easy for something like that to happen, especially if He didn't tell anybody. Thinking He was in their company, they traveled on before they looked for Him. When they became aware, and they did not find Him, they went back to Jerusalem to look for Him. After three days they found Him in the temple courts, sitting among the teachers, listening to them and asking them questions. His understanding and His answers amazed everyone who heard Him. We don't know what those questions were or what was being discussed. We don't know what questions they asked of Him. But there was a lively conversation going on and the listeners were enthralled. This young boy amazed them. How does He know this stuff?

When His parent saw Him, they were astonished. It was the question of the ages.

His mother said, "Son, why have you treated us like this? Your father and I have been anxiously searching for you." This is another one of Mary's words, and I find it interesting.

And he responds here, "Didn't you know why were you searching for Me? Didn't you know I had to be in My father's house?"

But they did not understand what He was saying to them. Now obviously He wasn't talking about Joseph's house. He made a different reference. Today, we know what He is talking about. But at that time, they didn't get it. They went down to Nazareth, and He went with them, and was obedient to them, but his mother treasured all these things in her heart. There she goes, doing that treasuring thing again. She didn't try to explain it or excuse it or whatever.

I don't have a good explanation for why Mary didn't connect the dots. She was told that she carried God's son. I also don't know why later His disciples didn't connect the dots that He would die and rise again in three days. It was only after He actually died that they realized what He had told them. With the disciples, there was some pride there, but that was not Mary's problem. I think she was still processing it and this kind of caught her off guard.

Maybe Mary and Joseph didn't connect the dots because until this time Jesus was a normal boy. Speaking of which, there is a so-called Gospel of Mary out there somewhere that relays stories of him playing in the sand and making pigeons, and they fly away. All of that is extra biblical. Nobody in that time ever thought it was biblical at all or Scripture. We don't know how "normal" He was. He was probably just like other little boys. He might not have been mean or done the mischievous things some little boys do. Keep in mind something else. They were writing the New Testament with their lives. They didn't have it as a textbook already there to read and see what they should do, know, or think. This was brand new to them, even to Mary, even though she had been told ahead of time. Elizabeth confirmed it, and other events took place, and she saw all these people who somehow knew about the birth of her Son. The angel showed up and told the shepherds and the Magi came from the East, and so on.

And Mary treasured and pondered still. That's the response here: They find Jesus in the temple courts; she treasured and pondered in that same way. We hear, "And Jesus grew in wisdom and stature and in favor with God and men." Someone raised the question, "If Jesus was 100% man and 100% God, how did He become in favor with God if He is God?" Not all aspects of Jesus concern His humanity, and not all aspects of Jesus concern His divinity, so Jesus as the Son of Man could certainly find favor with God. Well, Jesus, the boy found favor with God. Remember what I said earlier about Him playing in the sand and making pigeons and things? He didn't really do that. I mean, there are folktales about stuff like that, but nobody really saw or witnessed it. There is no real credible record of it, probably mostly in the realm of fiction that we read now, and people fictionalize history. That's the first part.

Also, because He started out as all man. At age 12, He knew there was something different about His Father's house and He needed to be there. I suspect that is the beginning of the Son of Man's coming into an awareness of who He was. We consider Him to be all God and all man, but He wasn't 100% all God and all-knowing from the beginning in His human state. He had to experience things as a human being, from a human perspective, in order to do what He had to do later. I have two books, one called *Fantasia Mathematica* and the other one called *The Mathematical Magpie*. And they are two books that are full of short stories based on mathematics. (I was a weird kid.)

One of those stories was about a two-dimensional world and one of these two-dimensional people had an idea like, "What if we could somehow move that way?"

The response was, "Oh, we can't do that, you can't do that, don't think like that, that's just preposterous."

"But, of course you can. We are two-dimensional creatures who didn't think of it as two dimensions, but we are what we are. Don't try to think of things that just can't be."

And then suddenly a three-dimensional creature intervened, and they had some interactions and everybody said, "You are right, there is a third dimension."

That's a simplified version of the story. But later, when I became a Christian, because I wasn't a Christian when I was a kid, it was kind of the same thing.

What better way for a three-dimensional being to explain three-dimensionality than to enter the two-dimensional world and say, "Here is how you get there. I am the way, the truth, and the life, no man can come unto the father except by me," and preposterous things like that. He had to be totally immersed in this world in which we live, right from the beginning. It was baked into Him, so to speak. It was part of every fiber of His being and growing experience.

And then later, awareness grew, starting somewhere obviously around 12 years old, when He was in the temple and began exploring. Of course, it made little sense to them because His father was Joseph and His house was in Nazareth. They went on their way. She pondered, and He grew in wisdom, stature, and in favor with God and men. God blessed and enabled all the things Jesus would do as He grew in life, but Jesus, the boy, didn't know everything God the Father knows. The adult Jesus would later say in Matthew 24:36, "But about that day or hour no one knows, not even the angels in heaven, nor the Son, but only the Father." While the context is the last days, the fact remains that the Father reserves certain information for Himself. Mary pondered and treasured those events and their significance in her heart. She got a preview from Gabriel the angel, and perhaps she had some inkling of how things would look for her adult son when He came into His full earthly ministry.

Fast forward to the last episode in Jesus' ministry in the Garden of Gethsemane prior to His crucifixion when Jesus said, "Father, if it be thy will, take this cup from me." You know what He is talking about? In the movie, "The Passion of the Christ," there is a scene at the beginning in the garden where a shadowy creature approaches Him. We don't have a record of that actually happening, that was a movie. Two people were there in the garden, the Son of Man, and the Son of God. Breaking down the passage in Luke 22:42, the Son of Man prayed desperately, "Father, if you are willing, take this cup from Me." But then the Son of God continued the prayer, "yet not My will, but Yours be done." This is where the full culmination of the Son of God and the Son of Man find themselves in this amazing tension for all the ages and all eternity.

Hematohidrosis is a physiological condition when under extremely intense stress, capillaries burst and blood will literally flow out of the sweat glands and ducts on your skin. It will appear that you are sweating great drops of blood. This is the medical description explaining the event reported in the account of Luke 22:44, "And being in anguish, He prayed more earnestly, and His sweat was like drops of blood falling to the ground." This had to be an amazing and incredibly difficult time in His passage. Why? Because my sin was all over him, and so was your sin. How many people do we have on Earth today? There are 331 million in the United States alone; nearly 7.9 billion in the world. Over the ages, how many billions more have gone and died before us? All of that is part of what He bore on the cross. That's a lot for three nails to hold up. That's a lot to walk around without staggering and collapsing out of the garden, under guard. There were tremendous spiritual tidal forces that were epic and flowing. This was momentous, from the time the Father said to the serpent, "her Seed will crush your head."

Over two-thousand years ago, this Boy, then this Man, struggled with who He was. About 300 years later, in 325 AD, a council was held in Nicaea. Those gathered at the council had a main issue, and that was whether Jesus was a created being or was indeed God and therefore equal to the Father. The latter assertion was adopted, thus establishing the doctrine of the Trinity. The Nicene Creed is a statement that came out of these great meetings in the early church. This was occasioned, at least in part, by the first real challenge to the church due to the influence of Gnosticism. Gnosticism had a different view of the world and existence. And the Gnostic influence into the church and the Gospel took the position that divinity came down and settled upon the man, Jesus. And then when they crucified Him, divinity immediately returned to the divine. For divinity and flesh to intermingle in the slightest degree, would absolutely ruin divinity, and that could never happen.

First, that would make the crucifixion of Christ without worth or meaning. And second, it does away with the resurrection from the dead. One place this became a genuine issue was the church of Ephesus. John, you may remember, was the one whom Jesus loved. He was later exiled on the isle of Patmos, and after that became the Pastor Emeritus of that church in Ephesus. He wrote three epistles, and of the false teachers he said, "even now many antichrists have come... they went out from us." (1 John 2:18-19, NIV) The false teachers who had come out from among them was a reference to people within this body of believers in Ephesus who embraced this Gnostic teaching, and allowed it to modify their understanding of the Gospel as they had received it in pure form from Jesus and His apostles. As a result, they had to be turned out as false teachers. And later in 1 John Chapter 4:1-3:

> "Dear friends, do not believe every spirit, but test the spirits to see whether they are from God, because many false prophets have gone out into the world. This is how you can recognize the Spirit of God: Every spirit that acknowledges that Jesus Christ has come in the flesh is from God, but every spirit that does not acknowledge Jesus is not from God. This is the spirit of the antichrist, which you have heard is coming and even now is already in the world."

Who is Jesus Christ? Just what's His name? The Son of God? No, that's not His name, that's His title. Jesus's name wasn't Christ. The Son of Man was named Jesus. Christ was His title. Jesus was the Christ. He held the position, the responsibility, with the title of the Christ. And John carefully words this when he said, "Every spirit that acknowledges that Jesus Christ has come in the flesh is from God" There are basically five things in that seemingly simple statement. In order:

1. every spirit that voluntarily acknowledges
2. that the acknowledgement is of Jesus
3. that Jesus is the Christ
4. that Jesus Christ has come, and
5. that He has come in the flesh.

Next John writes, "but every spirit that does not acknowledge Jesus is not from God." Note that John only includes Jesus in this second clause. The spirit that is from God must fulfill all five elements mentioned first, but the spirit that is not from God fails only on acknowledging Jesus, the Son of Man.

Why is that important? Because Jesus is the focus of all that other stuff and Gnosticism ripped that apart. Jesus, the man, was just a man falling in a hole in the ground, that's it, he is done, no resurrection, no nothing. Paul wrote in 1 Corinthians 15:16, "For if the dead are not raised, then Christ has not been raised either." And later in verse 19, "If only for this life we have hope in Christ, we are to be pitied more than all men." And that's what Gnosticism sought to do right from the beginning.

They had the first great meeting later on after the apostles died, and the first big challenge was the resurgence of Gnosticism. And out of that meeting came the decision that arose from the questions regarding the divinity of Jesus Christ. The creedal statements allow people who couldn't read or write to memorize a brief statement of "what we believe." It wasn't some mumbo-jumbo that you said that made you a Christian. It was a portable way that everybody could immediately understand and express to others what they believed and why they believed it.

Need closing prayer

# Chapter 2

# Sermon on the Mount: The Beatitudes

*Father, in Jesus' name I ask you, Lord, to touch our hearts and our minds. I pray, Father, for your Holy Spirit to work, and to allow our hearts to absorb, and to hear, and to receive what Jesus had to say in the Sermon on the Mount. We ask this in Jesus' name. Amen.*

In Matthew Chapter 5, verses 3-12, we find the Beatitudes, the first part of the Sermon on the Mount. We will look at some of the original language as we go through this. We are going to start with, "Blessed are the poor in spirit, for theirs is the kingdom of heaven." Now let's look carefully at language and words. Throughout the Beatitudes, we see Blessed. Blessed means full of joy or joyful. And it basically is a wish for, or a result of, receiving from God, His blessings. When we read, "Blessed are they who are poor in spirit," He is saying joyful or full of joy are those who are poor in spirit. "Theirs is the kingdom of heaven," is the result of that state of being. It is partly an attitude, but more than that, a state of mind, but more than that, the blessing is the fullness of joy by being poor in spirit.

As we as we look at this passage and look at other passages through the course of this *Jesus Said What?* series, we see that language plays an important part and we will see especially that, when Jesus spoke, He said things that had specific meaning in terms of what we need to understand.

In this passage, "Blessed are the poor in spirit," doesn't mean people without money necessarily, but people who have a sense of self-worth that is not higher than it should be. In Matthew

Chapter 5, the third verse begins this tour through the Beatitudes that Jesus talked about.

People who are poor in spirit are people who don't have an inflated sense of self-worth. They are not all caught up with "look at me, I am really cool guy Joe Christian. I am really special." Those who are poor in spirit don't depend on the wealth of their own spirit. They depend on God and recognize Him for who He is. And those who are poor in spirit, theirs is the kingdom of heaven or the kingdom of the heavenly realms. So poor in spirit is not a matter of wealth in terms of earthly wealth or being poor, but it is a matter of those who have learned that God is what's really important and central in their lives. And I believe that's why theirs is the kingdom of heaven. They are the ones who aren't cluttered by all the other cares of the world and the ones who can actually hear from God.

The word that we use for "poor in spirit," means to be not rich on my own account, not looking to myself as something that is especially high and mighty, but someone who acknowledges that without God or without someone else, I have no worth or intrinsic value in and of myself. "Blessed are the poor in spirit," then refers to those who recognize that they have no worth in themselves, their value comes from God, and they depend on God. As a result, "theirs is the kingdom of heaven."

When we look at the kingdom of heaven, this is another couple of words that mean something. Basileia means literally kingdom where a king rules, but of heaven. Heaven is worth noting here, because the word ouranōn is a reference to the heavenlies or the heavenly spheres. We find in the book of Matthew several references that talk about "for the kingdom of heaven is" and usually it's best to translate as, "the kingdom of the heavenlies." It is not the kingdom of God He refers to. In other gospels we hear a lot about the kingdom of God. But here in the Sermon on the Mount, Jesus is talking to those who had gathered, the crowds on the mountainside, and He tells them that those who are poor in spirit, who don't have an exceedingly high view of themselves, "theirs is the kingdom of the heavenlies," the kingdom of the spirit realms that surrounds us, and yet we can't see.

It's worth remembering as we go through this, that there is a king and a kingdom, but there are many things that are part of the heavenly realms, or the spiritual realms. We can't see angels, for example, and yet they are all around us. Neither can we necessarily see demons and the devil, and we can't see the Holy Spirit. We can't even see God, the Father right now. But all of them inhabit the kingdom of the heavenlies or the kingdom of heaven. So when He says the kingdom of heaven, the kingdom of the spirit realms belong to those who are poor in spirit.

The next item we will look at is, "Blessed are those who mourn, for they will be comforted." Now, this word mourning is a word that has to do with sadness, or a sense of loss. Often, when we mourn something, we feel bereft of something. We feel lost or by ourselves. When you lose a loved one, you mourn their passing. When you lose a valuable possession, perhaps you might mourn, that you can't find it. There is a sense of mourning that we cannot realize for all kinds of situations and circumstances. Blessed are those who mourn means that we abandon ourselves to those feelings and realize the loss we have without the person or without the thing or whatever it is, that causes us to mourn, but we can know that we will be comforted.

The promise here that Jesus gives those who are listening to him on this Sermon on the Mount, is that comfort is forthcoming. When we realize that now, the word here is the word paráklētos and basically it's the same word Paraclete that can also refer to the Holy Spirit. He's known as the Paraclete, literally one who comes alongside. When you are mourning and someone comes along to help comfort you, that person comes alongside and extends his or her arm around you over your shoulder. The term that is translated into English many times is comforter. It can also be other things as well, but the Comforter is the one, the comfort that He brings, is that same word. This word comfort is the same word that is used to refer to the Holy Spirit. Sometimes He will be a counselor, sometimes He will be a comforter. There are several English words that are translated from this word paraclete. This other word similar to it and related to it, parákletos, is a word that has to do with receiving that comfort, receiving the ministration of one who comes alongside. The implication then, is that there is one ready to come and extend comfort to you. When you mourn, you will receive what God has for you amid what may seem dark and distressful, those difficult to deal with moments in life that sometimes are difficult to comprehend. It may be beyond us why something terrible should happen, and the timing can be unexpected. We don't always expect to lose someone. There are other kinds of mourning as well where someone has been dealing with disease or something for a long time, and finally gives in and we lose them in death, but we saw it coming. Mourning can be immediate. An emergency strikes and it suddenly surprises us or it can be something that's a long time in coming, but mourning is something that God can help us with. As we mourn, the comfort of God becomes available to us. They will be comforted.

Another phrase we are talking about here is, "Blessed are the meek." Meek is an interesting word, especially in English, because it has a lot of different cultural connotations. It doesn't necessarily mean a buck-tooth kid who shies away from everything all the time. Meek doesn't mean somebody who is milquetoast; can't do anything, or scared to do anything.

For example, "Oh my goodness, I am meek and I am afraid of everybody and everything and I can't do anything."

But meekness actually is like those who are poor in spirit. It is a sense of not wanting to step forward, not wanting to put yourself first and lift yourself up, not wanting to be one who aggrandizes yourself, but one who will take a backseat or one who will be available to others, but not necessarily for his or her own personal self-interest.

The meek person will wait and let others go first. The meek person will allow others to take prominence or priority in situations. Meekness is a self-giving, self-sacrificing idea, without being wimpy. Meekness has to do with ready to minister, ready to be available to other people. And of the meek, Jesus says, "for they shall inherit the earth." Now the earth is a reference literally to the planet. Gē is the original Greek word here. It's the root word we get the study of geology, the geosphere. The world, the earth, is a physical place where we live. It actually refers to this sphere or this realm of existence, the world, the earth. When we look at it, "Blessed are the meek: for they will inherit the earth," the word inheritance is a strong word.

It's used by Paul in Romans Chapter 8, where he says inheritance is something we will have in common with Christ. We are coheirs with Christ. The inheritance we have is what Christ has. When we understand this inheritance is something that those who are meek can have, then we can understand it is something received from God at the hand of God. And we understand further that an inheritance is something that is often yours because of birth. "They shall inherit the earth," has to do with the spirit who will put others first and yet meet their needs and will step back in order to let others come forward to get their needs first.

Inheriting the earth means that eventually those who are meek are in a place where they will become the inheritors of all that is around them. It's not necessarily a bunch of riches and gold and jewels. But it is owning where you are, your sphere of influence. It's amazing how people who speak softly, eventually become listened to. And when people hear this softly spoken person speak, they will get quiet in order to hear what that person says. It's not always the one who shouts the loudest or shouts first, or speaks the fastest or whatever.

Often, people value the words of those who are meek, because they are few, they are quiet; they are well thought-out, well-reasoned, and they are compassionate. The meek will inherit the earth also has to do with the fact that respect will come their way because of who they are, and the way they live their lives and relate to other people.

Hunger and thirst are a subject in today's world. There are many places where there is famine, people who are starving. Blessed are those who hunger and thirst, only in this case, Jesus changes how He says it. "Hunger and thirst after righteousness, for they will be filled." We are not talking about food and drink in this case, and yet, the words referring to the desire for righteousness, are the same words for those who are hungry, those who thirst. Hunger implies that you need strength. Hunger implies that when you are hungry, you need to replenish that strength by eating appropriate food or whatever, but when we hunger after righteousness; that word righteousness means, literally, right standing or if we apply it a step further, in right standing before God.

The righteousness we are talking about is the object of our hunger and our thirst. When I was fairly young in my Christian walk, and as an adult, I became kind of stupid and tried smoking some marijuana. I immediately regretted it as a Christian. It was a bad thing to do; it was the wrong thing to do. And I sat there and tried to figure out *what in the world am I going to do now?* Then I looked over at my desk and a Bible sat there and my mouth literally watered. I was thirsty, and I broke open that Bible to Psalms, and I determined to read it until I read myself straight. I filled up with the word of God.

Some people read the text and believe that they were hungry and thirsty, because they stood up for righteousness and they were being punished, therefore they didn't eat or drink. I suppose that could be part of it, but certainly thirsting after righteousness and being hungry after righteousness can mean you are on the wrong side of the righteousness equation.

Jesus is not necessarily talking to the leaders of the Jewish faith; I don't know that the Pharisees and Sadducees attended it well. I think He was talking to common folk, because they were hungry for something. They had heard from others that this guy spoke remarkable words, and that He was worth listening to. They joined the crowds and followed them up to the hillside where they heard these words, "Blessed are those" [remember happy, full of joy] "who hunger and thirst after righteousness."

One issue we have is the fall of Adam, which led to sin. When the Pilgrims came to the New World, they came seeking freedom to worship God without a king or a queen telling them what religion they had to believe in. They had a rich but simple belief system that was a straight-forward trust in the gospel story in the Bible. Adam fell into sin, Jesus came to earth to lay down His life so that all who believed in Him could receive everlasting life. They used simple books called primers to teach their children to read. These primers introduced each letter of the alphabet with a simple rhyme that young minds could easily remember. The first letter of the alphabet, "A," was introduced with the rhyme, "In Adam's fall we sinned all." This simple phrase shows a fundamental truth that those pilgrims all believed, known as original sin. Every human being has inherited our sinful nature from Adam because of his original sin.

Those who have sinned and those who find themselves short of the glory of God, as it says elsewhere in Scripture, probably come to a place of repentance or at least with a desire to get back right with God. And they developed this hunger and thirst for righteousness, to get back in right standing with God.

A sense of weakness often accompanies the hunger we feel when we are physically hungry. If you have ever had any experience with fasting, you know fasting is not a simple thing to do. Most folks are in a habit of eating three meals a day. You spend half your day planning the next meal, because you sit at work or wherever you are. And you think, *I better not start this, because lunch is coming up, I better wait.* Suddenly, your work stops because you are waiting for lunch. You think about it, then make plans for it. The same thing happens at supper time. You say *it's about time to go home for supper.* Meals and eating and drinking are an important part of our lives, and habit builds them in. When you decide to fast, that means you will skip a couple of meals or a whole day, and suddenly, it's lunchtime and by habit, you end up going to the cafeteria or whatever, and eat your lunch with everybody else and then halfway through you realize *I was going to fast today.*

Now, God doesn't want to clobber you with a big old hammer or anything like that. But the point is, when we are hungry we feed that hunger with food, and when we are thirsty, we quench that thirst with water or something else. We are used to doing that; we don't even bat an eyelash or think a second thought about it. It comes naturally. The hunger and thirst for righteousness is being hungry and thirsty after right standing before God. We need to become where we are just as habit driven in our pursuit of righteousness, or right standing before God, as we are when it's time to eat a meal. The promise that goes with that is "they will be filled."

Here's an interesting thing I want to refer to in verse three. "Blessed are the poor in spirit for theirs is the kingdom of heaven." And then in Verse 4, "Blessed are those who mourn for they will be comforted." Verse 5, says, "they will inherit the earth." And verse 6 says, "they will be filled." And now in verse 7, we read, "Blessed are the merciful, for they will be shown mercy." The first one is in the present tense. And then the rest of these promises through verse 9 are in the future. "Blessed are the merciful, for they will be shown mercy." Mercy is something that goes hand-in-hand with the gospel of Jesus Christ. Mercy is not something we deserve. We talk about grace as unmerited favor. Mercy is forgiving someone when they don't deserve to be forgiven. I fall into that category. I think everybody does. Every human being has sinned before God, and none of us deserves mercy. But God has mercy on us, anyway. To be merciful means to show mercy to others. That means forgiveness, whether or not it's deserved, for "they will be shown mercy."

One of the best ways to receive mercy is to show mercy to others. People respond powerfully to mercy. I was doing some marital counseling with a couple. The wife had been in and out of counseling over the years in their marriage before I had ever met them and she had a lot of sessions with counselors where they told her to look at herself in the mirror and tell herself how wonderful she was and how beautiful she was, and so forth. It was all about making herself feel better about herself.

And I asked her at one point, "With all these times when you were involved with counselors, did any of them suggest that you forgive your husband?"

And she stopped short and looked at me with a strange gaze. She said, "What do you mean?"

I said, "To forgive him, to have mercy on him, even if you don't think he deserved it. Did anybody ever suggest that?"

"No, nobody ever said that. Nobody ever suggested that."

I said, "Well, that's what God did for us. That's what Jesus did on the cross. He had mercy on us before we ever deserved it. And yet He chose to lay down His life for us."

That's what we are talking about here. Showing mercy results in receiving mercy from God. And of course, that's the ultimate goal.

Earlier we talked about the poor in spirit. We talked about the meek. We have talked about the merciful. Here we see, "Blessed are the pure in heart, for they will see God." Here's another future promise. It's amazing how things in our lives can really overflow our hearts with negative stuff. It's been said that the things that you love are the things you become enslaved to. Paul said in Romans 6:20-22, "When you were slaves to sin, you were free from the control of righteousness. What benefit did you reap at that time from the things you are now ashamed of? Those things result in death! But now that you have been set free from sin and have become slaves to God, the benefit you reap leads to holiness, and the result is eternal life."

When we say be pure in heart, we are not talking about the bumpety-thumpety, the muscle inside our chest. We are talking about the part within us that needs to be pure. When something bad happens, you cringe inside, and it feels like it's coming from the heart. The Greeks had an interesting word for it, Schplanchna. Schplanchna means bowels of compassion. And when you have a pure heart, a bunch of extra considerations and concerns do not clutter it. A pure heart can look toward God without other stuff in the way. A pure heart is able to serve others without other considerations. It doesn't say, "I am going to do this because if I do, maybe he will do something for me." You don't do it because of something you are trying to gain from someone, rather you do it because, in your innermost being, you know it's the right thing to do. Maybe that person needs something from you, whether you need something from that person. It's not always about what we will get for doing or being some way to someone else.

A pure heart is a heart that does not allow itself to be loaded up with a bunch of distractions and things that lead us away from God, and away from where we should be in life. That's why it says "for they will see God." A pure heart that is unimpeded by other things, prepares to see God and prepares to look for God with the expectation of seeing Him. Blessed are the pure in heart for they will see God, is a powerful promise that shows that if our hearts are free from other things, we will see God and the sort of stuff that would keep us from God, will not bind us.

Peace is something we heard a lot about in the 60s and 70s. We have spoken about peace a lot in our cultural history in the United States. But another important aspect of this country is freedom. It would seem, though, that the principal thing for a long time was peace. I am not always sure that peace at any cost is the right goal or the right measure of what's correct or right in our culture. But the peace we are talking about here is something different indeed. "Blessed are the peacemakers." Blessed are those who will help make peace and keep peace between people. But peace as it's talked about in the New Testament is a sense of peacefulness. Real peace is an inward reality of settledness. Peace is not being all tied up in knots all the time, but being able to relax into the presence of God. It is being able to relax around other people in a way that doesn't have animosity and isn't worried about perception, etc.. Blessed are those who are at peace and able to help others to be at peace with each other. That's what this is talking about. Peacemakers are those who allow an atmosphere where everyone in that place can experience that same settledness and rest in their spirit. Jesus calls the peacemakers sons of God.

One characteristic of sons of God is that they will be those who make peace, those who help people come together. Peacemakers are those who stop fights, not start them; engage in things that will help people find their way out of difficult situations, not things that would contribute to them becoming further bound up into challenging circumstances. Peacemakers are those who help bring forth this sense of inner contentment that they can spend themselves on others instead of spending themselves in frenetic activity and fighting and being contentious. Peacemakers are the sons of God. God is in a lot of these Beatitudes. They will see God if they are pure in spirit, and they will be called sons of God.

The next one is, "Blessed are those who are persecuted because of righteousness, for theirs is the kingdom of heaven." We are back to the present tense. When He says "theirs is," it's not sort of, it really is. Notice all of these after the first one are in the present or future tense. Remember, the first one is, "Blessed are the poor in spirit, for theirs is the kingdom of heaven." Now we have, "Blessed are those who are persecuted because of righteousness, for theirs is the kingdom of heaven." It's the same promise. Isn't that interesting?

This is a present promise, like the first one. The poor in spirit receive the kingdom of heaven, and those who face persecution because of right standing before God receive the kingdom of heaven. The kingdom of heaven has to do with spiritual realms. If you want to ascend to the spiritual realms to be with God if they persecute you for righteousness, and you hang on to that righteousness, despite that persecution, that sets a place for you in the kingdom of the heavenly spheres with God. They are sons of God, but those who endure persecution for the sake of righteousness, theirs is the kingdom of heaven. There are more statements here that the Beatitudes usually include. And they continue with blessed. "Blessed are you when people insult you, persecute you, and falsely say all kinds of evil against you because of Me." That doesn't sound like a lot of fun to deal with. And notice how we are departing from "blessed are those who do this because they will get something." This is a slightly different direction. Blessed are you when people insult you, (not only when they are insulting you), persecute you, (not only when they are persecuting you), and falsely saying all kinds of evil against you. But here is the key phrase, "because of Me."

Often, if you let people know you are a Christian, they might insult you. They might make fun of you. "What are you, some kind of holier than thou?" "You think you are better than me?" That's often the response when you tell somebody you are a Christian or you try to talk to them about Christ. They may insult you, they may persecute you, which means constantly pick at you. When I was in the military, they stationed me in Army bands. In one such band, several gentlemen were always on my case. But I witnessed to people, and I didn't make any excuses for being a Christian. I talked to the commander of the band about the Lord, and I talked to the senior NCO. I talked to the first sergeant all the time. One clarinet player looked straight at me and said he was in charge of the rehearsal.

During the rehearsal he looked straight at me and said, "Can you play that a little quieter, or is it against your religion?" That was uncalled for, but he would do things like that to bait and taunt me all the time.

It was a well-known fact that I was a Christian and sometimes, when I look back, it probably made it easier to stay a Christian if people found out right away instead of tiptoeing around and waiting to see when they will find out. But if you live up to it and own it right from the beginning, they have nowhere to go and neither do you if you are honest about it. I always made it a practice when I went to a new unit, to not be afraid to let people know where I stood with Christ, right off the bat. Blessed are you when people insult you, when they persecute you, falsely say all kinds of evil against you, because of me. Look at our culture today. It's difficult to deal with some of these things because people do negative things to others to overpower them emotionally for whatever reason. Many people use this stuff for political gain or whatever. But it doesn't do any good in the long run, and it certainly isn't helpful. "When people persecute you, they constantly insult you, and say false things about you and you must defend those false accusations, blessed are you when people do these things against you, because of Me." When you own who you are as a Christian, when you own Christ as your Lord and Savior, you are likely to have some of these things happen to you. Understand that during that you can be happy and you can have joy. This sense of blessedness doesn't mean that you will feel good about the insults you get. It can be hurtful and difficult to live with. But it means amid it, you have a relationship with God, and God will be there with you to give you that sense of joy in His presence.

Paul had something to say about that in Philippians 4:4, "Rejoice in the Lord always. I will say it again: Rejoice!" And rejoice means literally to recycle joy. Sometimes you don't feel joyful about something in a situation or about where things are going or whatever. But then you can praise God and rejoice and renew your joy in Him. Is that what we always do? Probably not, but it's available. And God says right here, "Blessed are you when these things happen because of me, so that joy can still be yours despite these difficult things to deal with."

And then finally, the last one in these statements says, "Rejoice and be glad, for great is your reward in heaven, for, in the same way, they persecuted the prophets who were before you." Jesus doubled down on the promise that was stated at the beginning of verse 11, "Blessed are you" and then rejoice like Paul said, to recycle joy, and to rekindle that joy. Be glad because great is your reward when these things happen, insults and persecution, false accusations, and evil things against you. When this happens, that's the same way they persecuted the prophets who were before you. One translation says the prophets of old, but the point is when there were prophets raised up who spoke out for God. Look at what happened to Jeremiah, the weeping prophet. He had to spend months in the bottom of a cistern, which means he was probably standing in mud. It wasn't drowning, but to give you an idea of what it was like, the armies in World War I found out there is a thing called trench foot. The term came from trench warfare, where they would constantly slog back and forth in the mud. It would rain, but it would never drain away. Literally, they would pull their boots off and their flesh would come right off of their bones and their feet. The point is, when they thrust Jeremiah into the cistern, it was because he spoke words of truth. Isaiah had told the people of Israel to straighten up, to stop messing around with false gods and these other kingdoms, not to intermarry with people of other religions. He said if you don't stop, God will bring His judgment.

Jeremiah came along about a hundred years later and his job was to tell the people, "Okay, you heard from Isaiah. Isaiah told you what God wanted from you. He told you what God expected of you. And yet you didn't pay any attention to that. And you did these things, anyway. Now, that judgment of God is coming and Nebuchadnezzar is on his way, and he will take you captive into Babylon. That is God's judgment upon you, and will then become the tool that will draw you back to Himself, and He will restore you to Himself and bring you back to forgiveness."

It's an important concept that we need to get. "Blessed are you when people insult you, persecute you, falsely say all kinds of things, because of Me. Rejoice and be glad, because great is your reward in heaven for in the same way they prosecuted the prophets who were before you." Jeremiah had a tender spirit and a soft heart. He wept for the people of God, the people of Israel. People knew him as the weeping prophet. Isaiah had a hard job to do. He is the one who said, "If you don't straighten up, God is going to judge you." He didn't always have an easy time of it either. If you look at the Old Testament, you will see the prophets and what happened to them. It's like what Jesus told the people on the Mount, as He gave them this message, that is to be expected even now. When people find out you are a Christian, these things may happen to you as well. The same things that happened when the prophets before you came and were persecuted.

*Father, we thank You for all You have done in our lives and our hearts. Thank You for Your Word. The things that Your Son told us in the Sermon on the Mount are rich and full of blessing, wisdom, and understanding. I pray God that You would help these things become a part of us in our innermost being. Help us Lord to internalize and to own these words You have shared with us in Your Word. We thank You Father for all that You do and ask that You go with us now from this place. We give You praise and glory in Jesus' name. Amen.*

Chapter 3

# The Sermon on the Mount: You Have Heard it Said

*Father, in Jesus' name, we thank You, Lord, for all that You do, for Your direction, for Your wisdom, and for your guidance. I pray, Lord, that these words, spoken over 2000 years ago that penetrated hearts and minds then, would penetrate our hearts and minds today in a new and fresh way. We thank You, Lord, for what You do. And ask You, Lord, to guide our steps and guide our hearts and minds toward You, toward the throne of grace, and all that we do, in Jesus' name. Amen.*

In this chapter, we will talk about the "you have heard it said" statements of Jesus in the Sermon on the Mount, starting in Matthew 5, Verses 21-33. I want to preface it a little by saying that the Beatitudes were a kind of awakening, a wake-up call to the people of Israel, the Pharisees, the Sadducees, and the regular folks. They probably didn't fully understand the things He told them and probably had a different take on it. For all we know, the things He said were brand spanking new to them. And judging by their reaction and the things He said later, and their response to those sayings, He put them in a difficult position. Suddenly, He spoke with such authority as one who wrote the Book, which of course He did, that it threw them off their stride, and they felt like they had lost power. And what do human beings like to have more than power? What do they say, "power corrupts, and absolute power corrupts absolutely?"

When the Pharisees and Sadducees realized people were following Jesus and maybe ignoring what they had to say and the sermons they preached in the temple, they had some misgivings about His visit to Earth, shall we say. Here is a series of "you have heard it said, but I tell you" statements, and we will look at each one of them.

The first one, of course, is on the subject of murder. The New International Version says, "You have heard it was said to the people long ago, 'Do not murder, and anyone who murders will be subject to judgment.'" First, in the Ten Commandments, it says, "Thou shalt not kill," in the King James, but a better translation is murder. It's not necessarily talking about all killing. There is a great deal of thought and writing about the just war, sometimes to throw off evil, and you have to kill. God raised up armies and nations against each other in the Old Testament. Sometimes it was against Israel to correct Israel, and sometimes He would bring Israel against other nations to correct them. Our history in the biblical account and other accounts parallel to it are replete with examples of those kinds of things taking place. I would not hesitate to say that in any of those, God was in charge during that process, and He had a reason for it. I can't comprehend what His reason was in most situations.

Sometimes it's quite apparent. The chariots went out after the Israelites when they fled Egypt because, once again, Pharaoh had second thoughts and decided to bring them back. When confronted by a wall of fire, the Egyptians were stymied. There were enormous problems because of the pillar of fire by night and the pillar of cloud by day that accompanied the Israelites. When the fire halted Pharaoh and his army, they couldn't go any further, and they waited out the night. Next thing you know, they got drowned in the Red Sea.

You might have heard the story about the little kid in school. He always said, "Amen, Praise the Lord."

His teacher didn't like it much. She told the story about the Egyptian army being drowned in the Red Sea, and he said, "Amen."

She said, "Well, we know now that the Red Sea was really just a swamp."

He said, "Hallelujah."

"What are you yelling about now?"

"Well, God can miraculously drown an entire army in three feet of water."

These things happened. They are a matter of historical record. My dad, to my knowledge, died as an atheist. I grew up in an atheist home, and he said the Bible was an excellent cross-reference to verify history and historical events. But he denied any supernatural element of any of the stories that were told about miracles or anything else. Therefore, I would say that there is a fairly broad general acknowledgment of the historicity of the events in the Bible.

When God then got them out of Egypt, and they stopped at the foot of the mountain, Moses went up on the mountain and received the Ten Commandments from God. One of those was, "Thou shalt not kill." This is what Jesus was talking about when He said, "you have heard that it was said to the people long ago, do not murder." Murder is a more accurate understanding of the actual word used in the Ten Commandments. The issue there was murder, not just killing, because sometimes you have to kill in self-defense. There may be other times like when the Nazis overran Europe. Somebody had to go in and stop them. Unfortunately, sometimes killing, the taking of human life, is necessary. Usually, the righteous response is after the fact. Preemptive wars probably aren't such a good idea, but sometimes a just war is necessary.

The clarification Jesus brought was do not murder. It's not said, and I have seen nothing written, if the people had questions about whether any kind of killing was murder, but I know it was part of the law and generally understood. And then Jesus said, "Anyone who murders will be subject to judgment." That word judgment means the eternal consequences after death that you incur for such a thing. There is definitely some sort of judgment.

He doesn't stop with murder. He tells them consequences for other actions, using what we call a conjunction. Do you remember those? We learned about conjunctions as kids in our English language lessons. A conjunction connects and adjoins, but not necessarily "this and this." This is an exception rather than an inclusion. The exception conjunction used here, "you have heard it said, but I tell you, that anyone who is angry with his brother will be subject to judgment."

And then Jesus added, "Anyone who says to his brother, 'Raca' is answerable to the Sanhedrin. But anyone who says, you fool, will be in danger of the fire of hell." Somebody is probably thinking, *what's the difference?* The word in the original language gives us the tell. The word raca is a term from their local language. It was used to call somebody foolish or kind of dumb skull. But it was a different word than the original Greek word that was used when "thou fool" appears in the King James or "you fool" in the New International Version. That word actually implies, "You are such a fool that God made a mistake by creating you." To call somebody a fool is to say that God made a mistake which would blaspheme God. To claim that is to do something that only God is qualified to say. Now, does anybody think God makes mistakes? Sometimes, I want to think so, but He doesn't. He is infallible, omnipresent, omniscient, omnipotent, and so on..

Mistake is not in His nature. It is not in His intention for us or for anyone else. To call someone, "you fool," that word means literally, "you mistake of God." God made a mistake when He created you. That's a pretty dangerous thing to invoke over anybody. That's why He says the second one will be in danger of the fire of hell. The first one was a kind of slang word used for somebody if you didn't like them and you would have to answer to the Sanhedrin, because they would discipline you. They would tell you to clean up your act. But "thou fool," He implies, you would be in danger of the fire of hell because you have accused God of making a mistake in creating that person to begin with.

It would have been better had God never created you. If we say something or someone is foolish, is that the same thing? Will we go to hell? I want to make the distinction that we are specifically referring to the original language. The original language in Greek is a different word. They translated every iteration of this word in English, and it doesn't imply the same thing as the original word. Because if we say somebody is foolish, we could mean something as benign as you are silly or you are foolish to drive your car into that wall and kill three people. Both of them are foolish, and there is a wide range of what it can mean. But none of them truly call God and His creation into question per se.

Raca is literally the word in the original language, it's actually an Aramaic term, it's not Hebrew. You may have heard of Aramaic as a language. It was a sort of derivation of a slang version of a language that they used then. It's like an anathema thing that no one should use. We have literal translations to help us understand the best English translation of the Greek word, or in the Old Testament, the Hebrew word. But sometimes we need to realize that every time we hear that same English word, it may carry different connotations, and we have to pay attention to context. That's the text within the text. I taught, *Living by the Book*, a while back, and that's basically a church version of hermeneutics, which is the study of how to interpret Scripture properly. Hermeneutics can apply to a lot of things, but it always has to do with interpreting. When we interpret Scripture, one thing we must pay attention to is, who wrote it? What was their lot in life? When Matthew wrote this, what was he? He was a tax man. The tax man cometh. Matthew was basically a CPA; he was detail-oriented. He did detailed record keeping, and he cross-referenced these things Jesus said, and when Jesus had fulfilled prophecy by saying or doing something, Matthew was careful with his use of language, as was Paul. Mark was a little looser with his language. Luke was not even a Jew. But he was a highly educated, smart man, who had a fairly good and complex command of the Greek language when he wrote. When we carefully choose and use words, we must understand the care with which people used them and not twist them to fit our language today. Doing that would amount to us suggesting that if you said someone is foolish, it means that person is going to go to hell. That doesn't track. That would be what we call, eisegesis, which has nothing to do with the name Jesus by the way. With exegesis, "ex" means literally to dig out something from underneath like you would excavate a field. Eisegesis means to read something into something. We want to allow Scripture to teach us; we need to dig out what it is saying to us. Sometimes we fall in the trap of trying to take what we understand or assume and impose it on what we read in Scripture and proof text people and things like that, which is problematic.

There are two approaches. We call the first inductive, meaning that we learn from. The second is deductive, we assume a truth, take the facts and try to prove our truth. We work our way backwards to what we assume is the truth. Now, deductive reasoning can be helpful when you do forensics and try to solve crimes. You know, someone committed a crime therefore you take the facts and work your way back to the original act to find out how it happened. But when you are trying to learn from the Scriptures, you must understand who said what. Matthew was pretty smart. You don't get into a job like that without having something on the ball. By birth, he was Jewish. He well understood the history of prophecy. That's part of it. Now to whom did he write this? He wrote this to people who needed to hear this information, but primarily to other Jews who needed to hear that their Messiah had come.

Understanding those two things helps us realize that he may have assumed some things that other readers who are not from a Jewish background may not quite understand. That could be why He simply referred to "you have heard it said a long time ago do not murder" Yes, you have heard that because you are all Jews reading this, and you know that's in the Ten Commandments, but not everybody knows that. If they didn't grow up with the Old Testament, or at least with the Bible in the Christian church, they may not know that "thou shalt not kill" is in the Ten Commandments.

To understand what He was saying, He was trying to help the Jewish people understand what the original word really means. He clarified it by using an illustration. The first illustration was to call somebody raca. It was like saying, "dummy, why did you do that?" But to call somebody "you fool," says it would have better been better if God had never created you. That puts you in the position of judgment over another human being, which is God's prerogative and God's alone. That's pretty powerful.

He continues, "Therefore, if you are offering your gift at the altar and there you remember your brother has something against you, then you need to leave your gift there in front of the altar, go first, be reconciled to your brother, then come and offer your gift." Now in Mark Chapter 11, there is a similar passage, and Jesus says, "if you have something against your brother, then you need to go to your brother and forgive him so that God will hear your prayer when you go into the temple." We just saw two sides of this. What is your job, if somebody has something against you? You go to your brother and ask forgiveness. What is your job if you have something against someone else? You go to your brother and forgive him. No matter which side it is, it's your responsibility to approach the other person and either seek forgiveness or offer forgiveness.

What if everybody actually did that? What would happen to our world? Instead, we blame, we undercut, we tear each other down, and all kinds of weird stuff. The problem is, we just don't get it. It literally interrupts our relationship with God. If you are in the temple, go first and seek forgiveness, and then God will receive your gift. If you go to pray, go first and forgive your brother, then God will hear your prayer. Now they are not exactly the same, but they are similar. The principle I told my daughter- and son-in-law when they got married is marriage is not 50:50; marriage is 100:100. Both of you always give everything to your spouse. And if you follow that as a general principle, it will save a lot of heartache and pain. And that's the truth. If you have made that a rule in your marriage, you might last as long as we have, 45 years at the end of November. I think that's cool. And it's an exception in our culture today. And the closer you get to Hollywood, the worse it is, but there are some there whose marriages have lasted a long time, too, so you never know.

Next, Jesus tells us to settle matters quickly with our adversary, who is taking us to court. We are still talking about strife and disagreements with each other. "Settle matters quickly with your adversary who is taking you to court. Do it while you are still with him on the way, or he may hand you over to the judge, and the judge may hand you over to the officer, and you may be thrown into prison. I tell you the truth, you will not get out until you have paid the last penny," (Matthew 5:25-26, NIV).

There are a couple of things here. This example automatically assumes some sort of financial quarrel. But the point is to settle matters quickly with your adversary who is taking you to court. Today, our process is a lot more complex, and you get served papers and things like that if somebody is going to "take you to court." It was a more straightforward process in that day and age. Since the days of Moses, there were people who would sit and adjudicate the issues people had. As you may recall, when Moses was leading the Israelites in the wilderness, people came to him all day long, and he regularly interpreted the law to answer their questions and disagreements.

Finally, his father-in-law said, "Look, you are just one guy. You can't do this. You've got to delegate it." And ever since that time, in their culture, there were people whose job was to sit in adjudication over quarrels and issues that people had and could not amicably resolve themselves. Solomon did the same thing.

You remember the time where he said, "Okay, cut the baby in half?" Then he immediately knew who the mother was when she said to give it to the other woman.

Jesus is saying settle matters quickly with your adversary who is taking you to court while you are still on the way. Or he may hand you over to the judge. Your adversary knows the details from each perspective, and the judge will look at it for the first time. Wouldn't it be better for the both of you who are familiar with it to figure out a solution than to let some stranger who knows nothing about it settle it? You may end up on the right or the wrong side. And both people may end up being unhappy, so there is a practical side too.

Here's the next one:

> "You have heard that it was said, 'Do not commit adultery.' But I tell you that anyone who looks at a woman lustfully has already committed adultery with her in his heart. If your right eye causes you to sin, gouge it out and throw it away. It is better for you to lose one part of your body than for your whole body to be thrown into hell. And if your right hand causes you to sin, cut it off and throw it away. It is better for you to lose one part of your body than for your whole body to go into hell," (Matthew 5:27–30, NIV).

"You have heard that it was said, do not commit adultery." That's in there too, isn't it? But I tell you that anyone who looks at a woman lustfully (obviously assumes it's a guy) has already committed adultery with her in his heart. Jesus did something here that is, in many ways, quite amazing. In just a few words, the bottom line is, He tore down the entire legalistic process by which the Pharisees and the Sadducees exerted their control over the Jewish people. They would obey every jot and tittle of the law to the smallest degree. It was against the law to travel far on the

Sabbath, and there was a rule that said you could only travel so far from your property, then you had to stop. They figured out ways that would circumvent the law. I guess they would work around it or work through it.

One example is you could only travel so far from your property on the Sabbath. If someone had to travel further than the rules would allow, they could take along a bundle of stakes. They would take one out and either poke it in the ground or lay it down as they went along. Since they could consider the stakes their property, the only limits to the distance they could travel was how many stakes they could carry. And the length of the journey you needed to make on the Sabbath would determine how big a bundle of your stakes you had to take with you. That sounds crazy to us, but they wanted to be careful and stay within the legal limit of the law.

There were many rules in Jesus' day that they sought to obey. The elders would sit around and ponder little tiny points of the law and decide how to work their way through them for the law to be followed appropriately. The people knew this as the Midrash, an ancient commentary on the Law. And they came up with literally thousands of lines of stuff that make the Bible look small by comparison.

The leaders had a rule or a law for everything, far more complex even than you will find in the books of Leviticus or Deuteronomy in the Pentateuch, the first five books of the Old Testament. They laid down detailed rules, and that was only one example they came up with to figure out how to work their way around the law, and still be within the law. They would sit down, and one would say, "a passage says this," and then cross-reference another passage. This process would continue endlessly. They would get into these long and convoluted discussions and come up with rules. This was the world in which the Sadducees and the Pharisees ruled in the Jewish people's religious culture. Often the Pharisees would go out with their prayer shawl over their shoulders. They timed it so when the call to prayer went out, suddenly they would fall on their knees and pull their prayer shawl over their heads and loudly and vociferously praise God. They wanted to be seen. This was a culture of appearances, it was a culture of minutiae, and minute attention to details of law, and pointing fingers and demanding consequences. There was a lot of that woven into the fabric of their culture. When Jesus came along, He had a lot of unweaving to do. He really turns this one on its head. Do you remember the story of the woman caught in adultery? Some might ask, "Why was the woman dragged in front of the group of elders?" Well, back in that day and culture, women had little more of a right to life than a box of rocks.

For the record, I want to point out that women became very much an equal part of ministry in Christianity. Paul frequently refers to his co-laborers in Christ, including women such as Priscilla and others. He did not consider them to be lower than Him, but coequals. He used gender-neutral language. Many people look at Paul and think that he was down on women, but that is just not true. That comes from a misreading of Scripture.

Back to the question, "Why was only the woman brought before the elders to answer for her sin?" Because he was a man. It's kind of like that in the Muslim culture today. If the man said this woman did something bad, then she's wrong, and she's going to get punished. If the woman says he raped me, then she has to prove it and have all kinds of witnesses. That kind of culture was part of the overall larger Semitic culture. Keep in mind that Islam didn't come along until much later, 600 years after Christ.

The larger Semitic culture wasn't only Jews, but it was also the nomadic peoples of that part of the world. Their languages shared a lot in common, as did their cultural customs that had to do with these kinds of behaviors.

The woman was easy to blame and easy to fixate on. But in fact, it takes two to tango. And here Jesus does two things. He turns the issue on its head because He said, "the man committed adultery when he looked at the woman with lust." The second thing He did was to say the sin precedes the physical act. See what I mean when I said, "Jesus said what?" In that culture and time, this was eye-popping.

"I tell you that anyone who looks at a woman lustfully has already committed adultery with her in his heart." Let me cite an example. How about David? He saw Bathsheba from afar, taking a bath, when he was on the rooftop. He was already dealing with it before the act ever happened. It wasn't just the act; there was a bunch of stuff that went with it. He made arrangements for their first liaison. Later he had her husband killed at the front by issuing orders to have everybody step back, and sure enough, he died. It's mind boggling, and yet God called David a man after God's own heart.

What does that tell us about some of these things? It was the practice long before Jesus came along. And they always centered it on the woman being at fault and having no rights of recourse. But Jesus turned it on its head and he said, "for when a man looks at a woman with lust in his heart, he has already committed adultery with her in his heart." That word heart bears a little attention here, because when we talk about that, it is in the sense of the midst of his being. When he commits adultery with her in his heart, amid his being, we are not talking about the pump in there going bumpity bump. We are talking about something entirely different. Therefore, in Verse 28, we are looking at "kardia autou," literally, "the heart of you." This is a reference to the emotional midst of our being, not the organ that beats in our chest. They kind of understood organs and the word kardia. But there was a different understanding because when you see the right man or woman, your heart skips. I mean, a lot of stuff happens, and it seems to center right there. That is what it refers to; they were not making a medical reference. When He says, "he has already committed adultery with her in his heart," He is saying he has already completed his sin within his innermost being.

Now we get to, "If your right eye causes you to sin, gouge it out and throw it away." How many blind people do you see in church? "It is better for you to lose one part of your body than for your whole body to be thrown into hell." What's He talking about? Is Jesus saying literally that you should gouge out your eyes? Well, that means you could only sin twice. Or you cut off a thumb or a hand like they do in Islam. There are those who practice that kind of thing, but that is not what Jesus is saying here. He uses what we would ascribe to hyperbole. Hyper means above as when you get out of breath by hyperventilating. You get too much oxygen, and suddenly you get light-headed and dizzy, and you want to pass out. Hyper means above, higher than something else, whereas hupo means below. Hyper is something that implies above and beyond. It is better for you to lose part of your body. He is using hyperbole here, saying that you don't literally gouge out your eye, but it's like that. If something is causing you to sin, get rid of it. Run away from it, throw it away.

You've got to deal with it. We all have to do that. It is important that we own our responsibility for sin. But in our culture, everybody is constantly trying to jettison it, throw it off on somebody else, pretend like it never happened. And where do we learn that? I have news for you. You ever looked at little kids? One of the first things they learn is the word mine. They will grab something from the other kids, and then they will have a big argument about it. "Well, who did that?" "Oh, she took it from me, it's mine." I am not sure at what point parents teach their kids to be selfish and grab stuff and stash it and say "mine," but they sure learn it. Nobody reading this has ever done that, right? Of course your kids never did that. Yeah, they do it all the time. Why? It's part of the human condition. Now were we wired that way to start with? No, but something took place in the Garden of Eden.

Earlier, I mentioned the phrase, "In Adam's Fall, we sinned all." The primers used by the early Pilgrims to teach their kids the alphabet employed biblical rhymes. Original sin refers to the sin of Adam inherited by every human being on planet earth. Sin is part of the human condition. When you clutch a toy, and the other kid wants it back, but you say "it's mine," it is because of the primal law of possession. The old saying is possession is nine-tenths of the law. It's in my hands, therefore, now it's mine. But that's before they understand ownership remains with the original person, not whoever grabbed it last. There is a whole complex process that's part of our formation, but human nature is such that sin is natural to us.

This behavior we are talking about is not something that's isolated and only one or two people ever did it in history. It's something that everybody in one form or another is likely to repeat. If your right eye causes you to sin, gouge it out and throw it away. That word sin is important. When we talk about sin, we are talking about something that separates from God.

And where is God? Everywhere. How can you become separated from God, except for a special place He created called hell? Is this little paperclip really worth going to hell over? No, get rid of it, give it back. Now, as you get older, it becomes bigger than just paperclips.

In Matthew 18, Peter asked, "Lord, even if our brother sins against us seven times, do we still forgive him?" In one version of the story, Jesus says, "Even if he sins against you seventy times seven in a day, you must forgive him." Now that's how many?

Four hundred and ninety.

Now if you take 24 hours times 60, you get 1,440 minutes. If you divide that by 490, I think it works out to something like once every three minutes. Can you imagine 24 hours? If you are in bed eight hours, then that makes it even more frequent; just under every two minutes. That's a pretty extreme requirement. Actually, two words in Greek are one after the other there, the first one meaning "seventy times" and the second one meaning "seven" which would more likely mean "seventy times and seven."

That would work out to 77 times, or once every 18.7 minutes. However, even that often would represent a pretty annoying person. Should we forgive our brother that often? Why would God require that of us if He was not also willing to forgive us, as well? The reason God does that is because of His grace. Grace is unmerited favor, not something we earn. We certainly don't earn it when we require being forgiven a gazillion times a day.

Paul said in Romans Chapter 6:1-2, "What shall we say then? Shall we sin more that grace may more abound? May it never be." He uses a strong negative word there. "May it never be." Maybe that doesn't sound strong, but it is such a strong negative that Paul is saying, "Don't even think that we should do something like that." What he is saying is, "Don't sin more often to get forgiven more often." We have the cart before the horse. We are trying to push it instead of trying to pull. What we are dealing with here is the fact that we need to be forgiven often. Sometimes you eventually get it right, and you don't do it, you don't step in the same stupid trap you stepped in before. Sometimes we never figure it out. Some people are old coots and they keep doing the same thing the same way. Kind of like me. I am a man of habit and my wife says, "There's your OCD going again." They didn't invent OCD till after I was born, so it's not true. It can't be.

Anyway, how long does it take to replace a bad habit with a good one? I have heard anything from seven to thirty days. Some people say, "If you do it every day for seven days" you will change a habit. Some people say, "If you do it every day for 30 days." But I will tell you this, you can't just stop doing a bad habit. What you really need to do is replace it with an equal and opposite good habit. Let's say I have a problem with too much ice-cream. I eat it all the time. What's an equal and opposite good habit for when I want ice-cream? Maybe I could go out on a bicycle ride. Or I could eat something healthy or have a broccoli cone, instead of an ice-cream cone. Either way, it takes a while to form a good habit, but eventually it will replace the bad habit. "If your right hand causes you to sin, cut it off and throw it away. It is better for you to lose one part of your body than for your whole body to go into hell." Jesus is doing the same thing again, and in both cases He is not picking peripheral things like hairs. By the way, everybody has tiny hairs somewhere on their head or somewhere else. How important is each hair on your body? It's inconsequential. Who cares whether it's really important, somewhat important, or somewhere in between? It might depend on where it is. Why? Now there is a certain pain that women endure on a regular basis, at least some do. They will pluck their eyebrows. Does it hurt when you pull a hair out? If you pull it out by its root, you don't feel pain, right? Have any of you ever not felt pain when you pull a hair out? Now let me ask you a question. Even if you are only a hair on the body of Christ, the nerve systems still connect directly the hair to the brain, right? Every single hair is important. Am I right?

Okay. Be advised this is true. He is talking about body parts, though they are more consequential than a hair. While they are all important, they are all connected directly to the head of the body, which is Christ. If you cross your leg long enough, what will it do? Go to sleep. Why? It cuts off the circulation. The blood stops flowing. And what happens then? Your nerves can't feel anything. They get numb and cannot communicate with the head. In the body of Christ, the blood keeps you in touch. You can't afford to stay out of touch. But the body is important. He talks about a hand and he talks about an eyeball. My goodness, these are not simple little things. He is saying if something is important, get rid of it. It doesn't matter what it is.

Then Jesus says, "It has been said, anyone who divorces his wife must give her a Certificate of Divorce. But I tell you, that anyone who divorces his wife except for marital unfaithfulness causes her to become an adulteress and anyone who marries the divorced woman commits adultery." They clean that up later again in the law, but where did this come from?

Who originated that? Moses. It was part of the law. He got tired to hearing it. Finally, he said, "Alright then, you have to give her a Certificate of Divorce." But here is the thing: God views divorce differently than we do. He has a whole different perspective on it. Are you married? Were you married? Maybe not yet. However, everybody knows what wedding vows are, especially if you have been to enough of them.

What is a vow? It's a promise, but it is actually far beyond that. A vow is a commitment, but they do it before God. And it is something that is seen by God, and God seals it. You are answerable to God in honoring the vows you take in marriage. I am assuming a Christian culture here, but that's what we are talking about. Christ and the God of the Bible have a different view of divorce than we have now. In our culture, divorce is kind of like cheap candy. You grab something and if you don't like it; you throw it away and get something else. It's easily entered into and easily discarded.

In the Jewish culture of the day and age of Jesus, He at one time gives the story of the wedding, the bride, and the groom. They had a much more complex and binding process that led to marriage. Before your marriage comes betrothal. This is after being engaged. In our culture you are engaged. You might hear, "Oh I am engaged, look, I got a ring," and then two weeks later, "Oh I am not engaged anymore. See, I don't have a ring." I mean, it's like choosing a flavor at the ice-cream shop. In the first chapter, we talked about Mary and said Joseph was going to divorce her quietly. You don't just get unengaged when a betrothal has taken place. It requires a divorce. People will find out. But God talked to Joseph, and an angel showed up and took care of business. Joseph had made up in his mind to be honorable to Mary. But when God verified what Mary had told Joseph, he stood by her.

Betrothal is a stage we really don't have in our culture today. But it's an important one because that's where decisions come about concerning dowry and the bride's family giving something to the groom's family, etc. A lot goes into betrothal and the process. Therefore, a lot goes into dissolving the betrothed relationship. When God looks at divorce and the entire process that goes into it, He is saying here, "Somebody once said, give her a divorce certificate, but I tell you..." Notice everyone of these has it, "but I tell you," which means you have heard this, but it ain't exactly true the way you heard it or the way you understand what you heard. And both can be possible, maybe the way you heard it, maybe the way you understand it or interpret it now. "But you have heard it said, 'divorce certificate,' but I tell you that anyone who divorces his wife," and then he gives one exception, "except for marital unfaithfulness, causes her to become an adulteress and anyone who marries the divorced woman commits adultery."

Elsewhere in the Bible, it says God hates divorce. "'For the Lord God of Israel says that He hates divorce, for it covers one's garment with violence,' says the Lord of hosts" (Malachi 2:16, NKJV). It doesn't say, God isn't in favor of divorce, it says hates. That's a strong word. Here, Jesus makes it pretty narrow, unfaithfulness.

Marital unfaithfulness is a pretty big deal unless you watch television or go to the movies. But I am telling you, God doesn't treat any of these things lightly. Why? They are relational. They have to do with our relationship with each other. And when inter-human relationship unfolds, it unfolds at deep and profound levels, especially when you are talking marriage. And what is the fruit of marriage besides children and a next generation?

By the way, did you know that the United States of America is now in a declining situation, in terms of population growth? We have a net negative population growth from natural birth. The average birth rate now will not sustain our civilization and its size. The population will shrink. Now there are probably a lot of reasons for that. I think a huge reason is that God is no longer welcome in our culture. There is a small church near where we once lived, and they have an enormous poster on the side of their church building which says, "Make Jesus Legal." I couldn't have said it better myself. There is a concerted effort in our culture today, by the way, to make war on Christianity. I don't want to get political here, but people of faith, in particular Christians, are no longer welcome in many parts of our culture.

There are problems in our culture. And I am going to tell you where I think it started, and that's in 1963, because that is when God got kicked out of school when the Supreme Court prohibited prayer in public schools. And since then, gradually, we have pushed God back further and further from our culture, Main Street and our society.

Anyway, God has a different view, and He does not take these things lightly, and things that are relational in nature need to be taken with proper gravitas and value.

> "Again, you have heard that it was said to the people long ago, 'Do not break your oath, but fulfill to the Lord the vows you have made.' But I tell you, do not swear an oath at all: either by heaven, for it is God's throne; or by the earth, for it is his footstool; or by Jerusalem, for it is the city of the Great King. And do not swear by your head, for you cannot make even one hair white or black. All you need to say is simply 'Yes' or 'No'; anything beyond this comes from the evil one" (Matthew 5:33–37, NIV).

Now there are a lot of degrees in our understanding of what this means when it talks about taking an oath and swearing.

What does it mean to take His name in vain? Some may say it is to slander God's name. But what does it mean to take something in vain? It's all about me. When I take God's name in vain, I am presuming upon His right to over something. When I say the GD phrase or some other thing, I basically condemn someone or something to hell as I were God. I will tell you that the mouth is one of the worst problems we have. James has a lot to say about that little tiny tongue that guides a ship and a little lick of flames, the human tongue, that flames the fires of hell. That's pretty powerful.

When we think about things like this, do not break your oath but keep your oaths that you have made to the Lord. "But I tell you." Here is that "but" again, that oppositional conjunction. "Do not swear at all, either by heaven, for it is God's throne." We say that and we like to do that and we like to posture and say, "I will never do that, by such and such, I will never do that."

We like to invoke things like that. But it's a vain practice. And it's a good way to encourage God's wrath. You don't have any authority. You are not God, and you don't have His authority to invoke anything like that. So will you do this? You don't have to give a big speech like, "I promise and if I don't tell you, you can cut off my left arm!" Many of us like to make big grandiose promises. But all God wants you to do is, just say Yay or Nay, and let your 'Yes' be 'Yes' and your 'No' be 'No.'

That's simple. Did anybody here make a white hair turn black or black hair turn white? Sure you can. Have you heard of "Just for Men"? I have never tried it, I wouldn't know for sure, but I heard it goes away.

Verse 38 says, "eye for an eye and tooth for tooth" That's in the Bible. But here is that oppositional conjunction, "Do not resist an evil person." How can you tell an evil person? Probably by what they do, which is often accompanied by what they say. It's definitely accompanied by what they represent. There is an evil thing in our culture today where some states are trying to say we should have abortion on-demand even up to a baby being born.

According to the laws that are on the books, once the baby is born, you are now talking about a human being legally. That is a thin line to cross, the other side of which might be murder or infanticide. That is an evil thing to contemplate and to impose as the law of the land. I don't want to get political, but I say that's something evil that we have to deal with.

"You have heard that it was said, 'Eye for eye, and tooth for tooth.' But I tell you, Do not resist an evil person. If someone strikes you on the right cheek, turn to him the other also. And if someone wants to sue you and take your tunic, let him have your cloak as well. If someone forces you to go one mile, go with him two miles. Give to the one who asks you, and do not turn away from the one who wants to borrow from you" (Matthew 5:38-42, NIV).

Does that mean we in the marketplace as Christians cannot disagree with these ideas or with these ideologies? No, it does not mean that. But resisting an evil person implies some kind of direct conflict, does it not? There is something happening directly to you at the hands of another who is evil, and God, Jesus, right here is saying, "Do not resist an evil person. If someone strikes you on the cheek, turn to him the other also. If someone wants to sue you and take your tunic, let him have your cloak as well." Now the tunic is the undergarment. But let's say it was some kind of sports team. You give them your cool sports team shirt, then you offer them your overcoat too.

Someone wants to sue you for your tunic, let him take your cloak as well. "If someone forces you to go one mile, go with him two miles. Give to the one who asks you and do not turn away from the one who wants to borrow from you." I'm not saying Jesus wants us to all be patsies.

He is not telling Christians to be patsies, to roll over, and play dead. What is He saying? If He says, "Do not resist an evil person," why not resist him? Let me ask you a question. Have you ever been a victim of a bully? I was when I was a kid. I know my wife was. We probably have all run into them. Why do people bully? Because they get a charge out of it and they feel powerful. If you have ever been a bully, would you admit it?

I can't speak from the perspective of a bully because I have never been a bully. When I was a little kid, I was easily cowed, and I was afraid to hit somebody because he might hit me back. I was a skinny little runt or maybe not a runt because I was tall and skinny. I was the skinny kid and people picked up on it. One time they dragged me out of school in the sixth grade across the street from the school, because they didn't want to stay on school property.

We got over there and they said, "Okay, let's fight."

I said, "I don't want to fight."

"Well why not? Are you chicken?"

"No, my dad said it takes a bigger person to walk away from a fight than to fight."

Believe it or not, that actually worked. I turned around and walked away. They scared me to death.

The second time I ran into a "come to blows" situation, I was a sophomore in high school, which was the first year in high school that year. There was a senior who really thought he was something and a bag of chips too. He had me out in the lobby of the high school's auditorium.

He said, "I don't like you and I don't like anything about you and I think you are (blah, blah, blah). You are just going to stand there and look at me, huh?"

I didn't say anything. And suddenly my head went limp, and I realized he had come up with his left fist and "bam," he hit me right on the side of my face. I stood there and looked at him. He threw up his hands and walked away. I wasn't a Christian, I didn't read the Bible, I didn't know this stuff, but what I am saying is, "do not resist an evil person." Don't give that person what they want.

Those are the only times I ever came close to getting into a fist fight, and I never lifted a hand either time. Thank God for that. And I attribute it to a moment when I was four years old. I was walking around lost in the desert with my invisible friend, Tom. I had a stick I used for a crutch and I walked around to the opposite side of the block. I hobbled down the street and this lady was out there watering her grass (it wasn't really a desert). And she said, "Oh my goodness, are you okay?"

I said, "Yeah, me and my friend Tom are lost in the desert."

"Oh, you must be awfully hot and thirsty, would you like some cookies and milk?"

She invited me inside for cold milk and I love milk to this day. I had some Toll House Chocolate Chip Cookies for the first time in my life. If you are allergic to chocolate, don't try them, but if you aren't, then they are good.

Anyway, she told me about Jesus. It turns out she was a Sunday School teacher in the local area. She asked me if I wanted to invite Jesus to come into my heart.

And I said, "Okay, how do you do that?"

She said, "Well, you just say, 'Jesus, come into my heart and forgive all my sins,' and believe as hard as you can." I didn't know what she meant.

I said, "Jesus, come into my heart and forgive all my sins." I didn't know how to believe, I literally scrunched up my face and just got all stiff like I was the Hulk.

And she said, "Do you feel any different?"

I said, "No."

"Well, you keep praying that prayer and you keep believing as hard as you can."

Finally, I left out the back door and went back down the alley to my house. I had never been that far away from home on my own in my life. And I would stop every few feet and ask Jesus to come into my heart and forgive all my sins and then scrunched up my face and did my Hulk imitation.

I walked in the back gate, and I walked into the back door of the house, which led directly into the kitchen. My dad came through the other end of the kitchen.

I said, "Guess what?"

Remember, my dad was an atheist. I told him what had happened, and he laughed it off.

"Yeah, some people believe that. It's just a myth. It doesn't mean anything."

But I was sincere in trying to believe what this lady said and do what she said. And I believe that's how God preserved me from that sixth-grade fight. That's how God preserved me from that high school kid that wanted to get into a fight. I believe God honors those kinds of simple undirected prayers.

> "You have heard that it was said, 'Love your neighbor and hate your enemy.' But I tell you: Love your enemies and pray for those who persecute you, that you may be sons of your Father in heaven. He causes his sun to rise on the evil and the good, and sends rain on the righteous and the unrighteous. If you love those who love you, what reward will you get? Are not even the tax collectors doing that? And if you greet only your brothers, what are you doing more than others? Do not even pagans do that? Be perfect, therefore, as your heavenly Father is perfect," (Matthew 5:43–48, NIV).

Notice how it places tax collectors at the bottom of the totem pole. They were traitors. These were Jews who collected taxes for evil Rome. People really saw them as the scum of the earth.

"And if you greet only your brothers, what are you doing more than others? Do not even pagans do that? Be perfect therefore as your Heavenly Father is perfect." Now that is an interesting word, perfect. But that word in verse 48, teleios, is the word out of the Greek. There is another word, Hagios, from which we get the word holy. The Christians became known as the holy ones, and the saints later became known as Hagiosis. But teleios is a different word. There is a little thin book called *The Christian's Secret to a Happy Life* by Hannah Whitall Smith. She illustrates this concept by talking about a tree that bears fruit. In the early part of the calendar year, the winter warms up and the wind blows and stuff happens and little tiny green things come out on the tips of the branches and then little tiny flowers blossom. Pretty soon, you get into May, the April showers bring May flowers. And May flowers bring fruit in June and we see little tiny green knots. If you eat them, it will make you sick to your stomach. But by the time you get through July and into August, and sometimes September, that apple that was a little tiny green knot, way back when, is ready to eat. It is delicious and we can say all kinds of good things about an apple right off the tree.

Teleios has to do with a kind of perfection that is a perfection for where you are at that moment in your life. That little tiny green thing, that little blossom, that little flower, that little tiny knot, that little green apple that you shouldn't eat because it will make you sick. That apple at the end of the growth season that is absolutely sumptuous, is perfect, teleios. It is a degree of maturity along the way that is appropriate for the seasons of your life. He doesn't use free from sin, hagios. Here, Jesus uses the word, teleios. And He asks every one of us to be perfect therefore as your Heavenly Father is perfect.

In every situation in life, there is a perfection to be aspired to. That's not some weird mystical thing from some other religion or something, it's simply that we realize God's perfection in everything and if we cooperate with it, then amazing things can happen. Be this way, be mature for where you are. Be teleios, complete as your Heavenly Father is complete. And there is a completeness possible in every situation.

*Father, we thank You for this time we have been able to spend together. We thank You Lord for this Word that You have given us through Your son. He came and turned this world upside down, turned the Pharisees on their ears with these words He said. And Father, I pray these things will continue to turn us on our ears today, and to overturn culture and society around us. Help us be an agent for that turning around and turning upside down, an agent for that bringing Your presence into our world, and for us to be a representative, not just in word, but in name and action as well. We thank You Lord and ask that this Word would seep into our being and that we would become a product of this word in an authentic way. We ask this in Jesus' name, Amen.*

*God bless you.*

# Chapter 4

# Sermon in the Valley

*Father, in Jesus' name we ask you to touch our hearts and our minds. We pray You would let Your word capture us and carry us back into that time when You spoke with Your people. Help us Lord to see that the human condition really doesn't change all that much. And that You are eternally the same. We give You praise and glory in Jesus' name. Amen.*

How many of you knew there was a Sermon in the Valley? We always hear about the Sermon on the Mount. And we chewed up a couple of big chunks of it previously. That one is in Matthew. Well, in the book of Luke, we have a somewhat different take. They went to a high place and then He taught from there. But in Luke 6:17 it starts out, "He went down with them and stood on a level place." That sort of sounds like they were going down a hill, and then they found a level spot, therefore, he stopped there.

"A large crowd of His disciples was there and a great number of people from all over Judea, from Jerusalem and from the Coast of Tyre and Sidon, had come to hear Him and to be healed of their diseases. Those troubled by evil spirits were cured, and the people all tried to touch Him, because power came from Him and healed them all" (Luke 6:17b-19).

That's a pretty good beginning to a sermon. They got close, and touched Him, and boom, He healed them all. We need to understand a little about the dynamics. There has always been what we would refer to as crowd dynamics. That's the ebb and flow, popular opinion and how people behave in smaller groups, larger groups, and as individuals, etc. But in that day and age, they didn't have the Internet, social media, TV and radio programs. They didn't have characters like heroes, favorite stars, stories, rock idols, etc. It was a different time and yet in many ways; it was the same.

What draws people to an individual? What do you think? Many people will say personality, charisma, and popularity. All kinds of things attract people. Personality is part of it. Charisma is certainly part of it. Jesus definitely showed personality when He got up there and started talking to them about some things in the Sermon on the Mount. But here, He will have a different approach. Popularity attracts people, but how does popularity occur? Success leads to popularity. Word of mouth leads to popularity. People get to know somebody and they talk to other people. Today we have the Internet and technology. But they didn't. Yet, it still happened, didn't it? People heard about Him, they found out about Him, and they went after Him.

Miracles are right up there as well. That's at the top. And you know what? That stuff works today too. In the early days of the Pentecostal Movement, the 40s, 50s, there were a lot of huge healing ministries. I don't remember his name offhand, but one guy set up shop outside of Chicago and the local doctors, the medical community, tried to have him arrested. Anybody want to know why? They charged him with practicing medicine without a license. He and the other so-called healing evangelists were healing people left and right in droves. The medical establishment tried to get the police to shut down the meetings. They prayed and people got healed. They gave back their crutches and wheelchairs.

What makes a person in this world successful? For one thing, it usually benefits somebody. Coming up with a new product or a better mousetrap or whatever leads to a better life. I mean, there are lots of ways to become successful. Success can be pretty broad. Some real hucksters can be successful. But we wouldn't say that was the same success Jesus enjoyed. Healing certainly benefits people. He came down with them and stood on a level place. An enormous crowd of His disciples was there, along with a bunch of people from all over the place: Judea, Jerusalem, Tyre and Sidon. They came to hear Him and get healed of all of their diseases. He cured people troubled by evil spirits.

People go after power. They pick up on where power is and they recognize power. People like that. People like positive things. And when you can bring the most positive thing to people, healing and deliverance, there is a power that actually can transform lives. That's something people are hungry for. And when they find it, they want it; they taste it, and they want more of it.

This was happening. He didn't need some advertising firm in downtown New York on Wall Street to tell everybody what a great deal He was. There weren't billboards and ads saying you need to hear Him, and on Friday, there will be a big healing at the civic center instead of a truck show.

Anybody can build up something, but it has to have substance to last. People who came to Jesus, I don't know if you would call it fun or not, but they were certainly getting healed. Can you imagine being part of the crowd and watching these things happening yourself? I get goosebumps just thinking about it. And if you have ever been in a huge revival where the Holy Spirit comes down, you get goosebumps all over.

People tried to touch Him because power came from Him and healed them. People were anxious and they wanted to get close. One of my favorite sermons to preach and favorite stories to share is the story in Luke 8:43-48 of the woman who had an issue of blood for twelve years. This woman had been off limits to everybody for years. Back then, if you had an issue of blood, then you were unclean and everyone you touched was unclean. She might as well have been a leper. She thought, *Jesus is coming my way. If I can just touch the hem of His garment. It's got to be better than this.* Nothing else had worked. All the doctors had tried for years and years. She struggled with her sickness and nothing happened. Suddenly, through the crowd, she went up to Him, and she barely touched His garment.

He asked, "Who touched me?"

His disciples said, "What are you talking about? There are people all over the place."

He said, "I felt power come out of me. Who touched me?"

And she said, "I did. It was me."

What happened was a miraculous moment. Instantly, He knew something had happened. His disciples didn't get it. She was basically thunderstruck, because He caught her red-handed. These aren't charlatan tricks or psychological feelings or anything like that. These are actual events that took place when they didn't have the so-called miracle of modern medicine. Don't get me wrong, there are tons of things in modern medicine that seem almost miraculous. But that started back in the day of the so-called Era of Enlightenment. That's when people tried to understand and study God's creation in an organized way. That was their goal, to understand how everything worked. They assumed God had a plan. They wanted to understand how He did all this stuff and how it all ticked. That's where science came from. Now it's a different enterprise, and you've got people like the atheist Richard Dawkins running around, telling everybody that God is not real. Now people try to use science to disprove God. It's amazing how fast the enemy tries to figure out how to turn something for his benefit.

There is a conspiracy going on. There is one conspiracy that is 100% true and the chief conspirator behind it all is the devil and his demons. That's the real conspiracy theory. That's the one that is true. Some people hunker down and they have all these different conspiracy theories about this, that, and the other. The devil sees what works, and he does his best as fast as he can to pervert it to his own ends and draw attention away from God toward himself. He is self-aggrandizing and everything draws attention to him and away from God. We need to realize that. Evil spirits got cured and people tried to touch Jesus, because power went from Him and healed them all.

I mentioned this when we touched on the word blessed, in the Beatitudes in Matthew 5, but I want to call attention to it and see if you remember what I said. In Luke we read, "Looking at His disciples, Jesus said, 'Blessed are you who are poor, for yours is the kingdom of God.'" Now the language there is slightly different, because in Matthew 5, "Blessed are those who are poor in spirit." Here, he says, "Blessed are you who are poor, for yours is the kingdom of God." Isn't that interesting?

He speaks to them in second person, "you." And, why poor? Are we talking about financial status? If we are talking about material things, why does being poor make the kingdom of God yours? Is it because people with more money tend to have more possessions, and the more they have, they think they did it themselves? Therefore, they don't give credit to God?

I would venture to say that if you are poor, generally speaking, people look down upon you. We see beggars on the street and we also recall the story of Lazarus and the rich man in the Bible. But we don't know people's situation. It could be they appear poor, but it could be the way they like to dress. Appearances aren't everything, but I guess it's how people view you, for lack of a better term. What's another difference between here and Matthew 5? "Blessed are you who are poor, for yours is the kingdom of

God," but in Matthew, "blessed are the poor in spirit, for theirs is the kingdom of heaven."

Do you remember what I told you about the word "heaven" or "heavenlies"? It refers to the spirit realm all around us. And Matthew talked all the time about the heavenlies and the kingdom of the heavenlies. He said heaven, but heavenlies is a better understanding because it implies the spiritual realm that is around us. Bad actors and good actors populate the heavenlies. There are angels and there are demons. When you have God, you have got the Holy Spirit at work. Jesus says, "Blessed are the poor in spirit, for theirs is the kingdom of the heavenlies." If you are a poor in spirit, you trust in God. And because you trust in God, He gives you power over the kingdom of the heavenlies.

When He said, "Blessed are you poor, for you shall have the kingdom of God," the people probably didn't get it right then. But what we need to understand is, being poor materially means dependence on God also, but in a material way. Therefore, the kingdom of God and all of its wealth, and all of its riches, are yours. It doesn't matter whether it's a spiritual kingdom or the physical kingdom, being poor in one or the other, opens God's doors of blessings in your life. In a way it's parallel, but it's also different. What's the difference? Every time you go to a different place, you have a different audience. There are a lot of parallels in this world. We could go to the hills of West Virginia, and what do people want to hear about there? There used to be a lot of coal mining there. It stands to reason someone would probably talk to them at some level they would understand and relate to them in their situation. There isn't a lot of money in coal mining these days. Some coal miners end up with black lung disease. It's understood that once you are there, you can't break out of it. There is nothing else you can do. Their children have that to look forward to someday. You might hear them say, "Oh, I get to inherit this from my dad. I will probably get the black lung disease, too." It's a bleak and dire kind of situation. Whereas, if you go to some place else, let's say, Detroit, the big thing there was motor vehicles, the United Auto Workers.

Wherever you go, you have a different audience and you need to relate to people where they are. Now, it's good if they try to relate to you where you are, too, but as Christians, it is important for us to learn to relate to people where they are. Jesus was a master of that. He knew where you were coming from before you knew you were even coming to see Him. In John 1:47-50, we read:

> "When Jesus saw Nathanael approaching, he said of him, 'Here is a true Israelite, in whom there is nothing false.' 'How do you know me?' Nathanael asked. Jesus answered, 'I saw you while you were still under the fig tree before Philip called you.' Then Nathanael declared, 'Rabbi, you are the Son of God; you are the King of Israel.' Jesus said, 'You believe because I told you I saw you under the fig tree. You shall see greater things than that.'"

Jesus speaks to them where they are. In the Sermon on the hill, or the valley, He talks to a different group, and therefore He relates to where they are. Whereas in Matthew when He talked to the people there, He talked about being poor in spirit and the kingdom of heaven.

Let's look at the next one, "Blessed are you who hunger now, for you will be satisfied." See what He did there? I am talking about a sequence of time of now and then, of present and future. There is something to look forward to. "Blessed are you who hunger now, for you will be satisfied." Notice that's not the next thing back in Matthew. In Matthew, He talks about mourning and meekness. Then He talks about hunger. But what does He say about hunger? He puts hunger and thirst together and says,

"Blessed are they who hunger and thirst for righteousness, for they will be filled." You see His focus is different here, where He talks about, "Blessed are you who hunger now for you will be satisfied."

Next we read, "Blessed are you who weep now, for you will laugh." There is always weeping and laughter. Here he talks about hunger and weeping. "Blessed are you when men hate you, when they exclude you and insult you and reject your name as evil, because of the Son of Man." Did you catch all that? I know there are bullies in this world, and bullying is bad. Bullying is terrible, and it's really sad when that happens. Kids are kids, and that's what they do sometimes. It almost seems like they read the book as soon as they are born, and it says, "Thou shalt go and thou shalt bully, or be bullied." This is a pretty powerful statement. "Blessed are you when men hate you, when they exclude you, and insult you, and reject your name as evil, because of the Son of Man."

Jesus is saying if you connect to me, these things may well happen, but in the long run, it's going to be a blessing for you. God will bless you amid this social trauma. They probably wouldn't have called it social trauma then, but that's what it amounts to. There is the emotional and psychological distress that goes with that sort of thing. I mean, how often can you get told you are ugly, stupid, clumsy. I don't want to be around things like that. It's difficult to ignore or overlook, especially as a child. I tried to be careful with my children. I would tell my son or my daughter,

"You know, that was a stupid thing to do."

They would respond, "I am not stupid."

"I didn't say you were stupid. I said what you did was stupid."

If we don't make that distinction for them, they will be on their own. They will own it as who they are. We must be careful with young people. But it can damage even adults.

And that's the problem with racism. My goodness, how much of that must you hear? It matters if all your life there's some sort of negative remark everywhere you go. You can't run away from it. You know, racism is a terrible thing to grow up with and live with. I grew up in western Colorado, and it appalled me. I saw the civil rights stuff on TV, but it was distant.

After I completed my training at the Army Navy School of Music, it dismayed me when I got to my first US Army Band at Fort Benning, Georgia. We went out to play for some kind of festival or Fourth of July celebration. On the way back, we stopped the bus way out in the parking lot of a restaurant, and the bandmaster and the first sergeant went in. About five minutes later, they came back out to the bus. The band commander stomped on to the bus and said, "Those stupid --" and some choice language including the word "redneck" flew out of his mouth. We started up the bus and went on down the road. What made him angry? He was told the African American band members would have to eat on the bus. They couldn't come in. Therefore, we all left together. I have never experienced being discriminated against because of my race and I can't for the life of me imagine what that must be like.

However, when you become branded as a Christian, that can follow you and cause problems for you. Are you ready to count that cost? Are you ready for when they hate you and exclude you and insult you and reject your name as evil, because of the Son of Man? For sure, are you ready to be ostracized?

I don't know if you have been paying attention, but there are some things coming down the pike that are insidious. We live in precarious times. People of faith are not always welcome in the marketplace. What does that mean? Now if you are a Christian, a person of faith, you are being painted in the marketplace as a bigot, as a horrible person, as a person to marginalize and punish, etc. It's coming, folks. Right now it's in its infant stages, but if you want to see what it actually comes to, read the Book of Revelation, especially the part about the Antichrist. What does he do with those who come to faith during the tribulation? He beheads them, among other things. We saw a foreshadowing of that with ISIS and the things they do. There is an appalling effort to exterminate Christians in increasing numbers all over the world. Countries like China haven't really let up. There are more Christians being killed daily than any other single group of people in the world. Religious bigotry has martyred more Christians in the last 10 to 15 years than since the time of Christ. If that's kind of an eye opener, it should be. That's where this is headed.

In a May 6, 2019, article in ChristianHeadlines.com Michael Foust wrote, "An estimated 80 percent of all persecuted religious believers around the world are Christians, according to new British report that also says the level of persecution in some areas 'is arguably coming close to meeting the international definition of genocide.'" A couple of months later he wrote in the same publication, "'It is estimated that one-third of the world's population suffers from religious persecution in some form, with Christians being the most persecuted group,' the report says, quoting data showing that in 2016, "Christians were targeted in 144 countries—an increase from 125 in 2015."

Blessed are you when men hate you, when they exclude you. Now what about that exclusion thing? What happens? According to Revelation 13:16-17, in order to buy or sell, the mark of the beast must be on either on your right hand or on your forehead. You might wonder, "Why can't I just get out a pen and draw a picture?" Well, it might come off, but maybe it's a different mark. Because over in some places in Europe, people have experimented with a subcutaneous chip implant, kind of like for pets. And if you don't have one of those, they won't take your money anymore. That's where we are on the way to. There are ways to do this that are insidious. It's great technology, but should we bow down to the god of technology? Somebody mentioned something about a search engine they now use and said they don't touch Google anymore. Someone said it in passing on television. But there is a lot of that stuff going on in big tech right now, too.

Google is easy to use, but here is my point. I work in high-tech in IT. I am a Network Security Engineer. I work on firewalls in the network environment. And I will tell you that the IT community leans to the left. I am a Conservative and I am careful about what I say to people. However, I am not afraid to tell people about Jesus and that I am a Christian. With politics or something like that, I kind of tread easily. We need to understand that these things we read here are prescient. That means they are forward aware or future aware. They are talking about things that will become reality. They have become reality many times and will become reality again. One of the huge places for that becoming reality was over in Germany during the Nazi uprising. People died for their faith.

Exclusion, insult, reject your name as evil, that is happening with Christians now. People of faith are being deliberately mischaracterized in the marketplace. I mean, the image of people of faith is being put across as evil and bigoted. That's exactly how fascists and communists behave. We need to realize and wake up. It is coming soon to a neighborhood near you.

"Blessed are you when men hate you, exclude you, insult you, reject your name as evil because of the son of man. Rejoice in that day and leap for joy, because great is your reward in heaven. For that is how their fathers treated the prophets." This is another "then and now," or "now and future" situation. We are looking forward to a reward in heaven. In that day when these things happen to you, don't get all mopey about it, get "leapy" about it. Leap for joy in that day. Rejoice. What does rejoice mean? How do you see that word rejoice? What does it mean to you? Some may say celebrate, be happy about it, "Don't worry, be happy." What does "re" have to do with joy? Keep doing it. You do it again. It's sort of like recycling joy. The more you do it, the easier it is. If you learn how to respond to those sorts of things positively, then it's going to have a profound effect on people around you. Did you know that?

I was in PLDC, Primary Leadership Development Course, in the Army, and we all got shipped off to Fort Knox, Kentucky. As a staff sergeant, and the senior guy there, I outranked everybody else at least for the first weekend, so they assigned me the role of First Sergeant. I found myself being constantly mobbed like Jesus, I guess, only I didn't touch anybody and heal them. But they crowded around me with all kinds of questions.

The first week, our superiors finally assigned squad leaders and platoon sergeants. That took the load off too since I could ask, "Did you talk to your squad leader?" "Did you talk to your platoon sergeant?" But there was another guy, and we managed our squads next to each other and got to know each other. I think it was through Chapel. We both were Christians, and we bunked down next to each other.

At some point halfway through the course, a couple of the guys came over to us and one said, "How come this stress isn't bothering you guys?"

We just looked at each other. I looked back at the questioner and I said, "Well, we both love the Lord, and we give it to Him. We know to talk to him about things."

And he said, "I knew there was something different about you two."

I am not saying that was persecution. When you are in the military, though, your superiors will ride you and make you do difficult tasks. It's not a simple thing to do. However, that was our response to the harsh treatment. That is how we came across and people saw a difference. When you learn to rejoice in that day, and leap for joy, that's something that can have a profound and positive impact on people around you. And guess who they will come to when they get stuck?

The Army once stationed me in an Army band in Frankfurt, Germany. We were at a beer fest, a kind of festival that's quite popular in Germany. Basically, it is an excuse to have a city-wide beer bust to go out and drink with friends all week long. They would invite US Army bands and we would play different German and American music at these fests. When we finished, we would put our stuff away and then everybody would go out and cut loose for a while. Band members would eat a hot dog or nachos and drink beer with the locals before returning to the barracks.

Everybody had dispersed to enjoy the fest, but I was just standing around when the Sergeant Major walked up to me, He had been drinking and was already a little drunk.

He said, "Sergeant Brown, I just want you to know I really admire you, man. I know you talk about Jesus all the time, and I want you to know that I hear you, man, I hear you. Keep talking about Jesus, it's coming through. I don't always show it... you know what I mean ...I mean you know."

In his own way, he told me he admired my fortitude in talking about Jesus. I never said another word about our conversation. It was kind of like our dirty little secret and he didn't give me the stink eye, if I looked at him. But I knew it probably wouldn't be a welcome subject when he was sober, the next day or whenever I saw him next. Hopefully, you get what I am saying.

When people find those moments of introspection, it's amazing what can happen. If you have been consistent in your walk and in your resiliency in responding to problems and issues in life, then that tells them when you have something that is real. When people find themselves stuck, they want what you have. Not everybody can do that, it's not a psychological thing. It's not a well-tempered psychology, it's a relationship thing. It about being related to Jesus. And that's exactly why, when they hate you, exclude you, insult you, reject you, because of the Son of Man, you can rejoice in that day, and leap for joy. When you rejoice and leap for joy, later on people will remember that about you. And that will give you an opening someday.

"Because great is your reward in heaven, for that is how their fathers treated the prophets." Now in Hebrews 11, the writer talks about those saints of old, that they sawed them in half. Can you imagine being sawed in half? The unspeakable things in cruelty that humans impose on each other are amazing. You turn the devil loose and he has a fertile imagination and can come up with all kinds of ways to hurt people. And you know Muslims, don't tell me they serve a God of peace. I am sorry, but the God of Islam is not the same as the God of the Bible. It certainly bears repeating when people walk around and say, "We all serve the same God." I suppose in a way that's true, because ultimately even the devil serves God and only serves at His pleasure. But to suggest that the God we serve in Christianity is the same God as in the Book of Islam, the Quran is not true. He is not the same God. He is mean and malevolent, and has other characteristics that the God of the Bible does not have. We need to recognize that. And all the way through the Old Testament, look at some of those gods they had to deal with. Some gods required you to sacrifice your first-born baby in fire. Nero lit Christians on fire for his pleasure, to hear them scream.

When you can rejoice in that day, people will recognize that strength and I will tell you that there is no psychological strength or mental attitude in the world that can overcome those things, all by themselves. It's just not possible. Rejoice because great is your reward in heaven, that is how their fathers treated the prophets. It's not new. They were awful to the prophets. Remember the Weeping Prophet Jeremiah? How long did he stay in the cistern's bottom with mud up to his knees? We get upset if there is a little dampness on the floor. He waded around in the cistern and when the king heard about it; he had him hauled up out of there.

Alright, so woe here we go. By the way, this is not a rock song about to start, "Woe, woe, woe!," but these are the woes. "Woe to you who are rich, for you have already received your comfort." We have long ago left the Sermon on the Mount. This is completely different. There are harmonies of the gospels. They try to "harmonize" every passage of Scripture in the four gospels. And there are some who in contorted ways have tried to force this Sermon in the Valley and the Sermon on the Mount to say the same thing. But I will tell you that Luke recorded a version that was specifically geared toward his audience at the moment, when they stopped on the way down the hill into the valley at a flat spot. He healed them and told them these things. And what He is saying is completely different.

"Woe to you who are rich, for you have already received your comfort." What does that mean? I suspect it has a lot to do with the ease with which rich people can become complacent and totally dependent on their riches and not ready to depend on God. Their riches become a replacement for God and indeed can keep them from God. "It's easier for a camel to go through the eye of a needle than for a rich person to get into heaven," Jesus said. Now somebody said, "Let's talk about this place and it's really small so the camels had to go through on their knees." Maybe there is a place like that, I don't know. But I think Jesus was using hyperbole, an extreme example to make his point.

Rich people, it's too easy to become dependent and self-sufficient in your own riches whereby you have no need for God, or so you think. It becomes too easy to believe that you have no need for God. Some of the most amazing saints I have known, however, were rich. I knew a guy who owned three or four of the high-rise hotels along the oceanfront in Virginia Beach, Virginia. His name was Charles. He went shopping and bought a 450 SEL, two-seater Mercedes for his wife's birthday, and paid cash. This guy was well off. He also volunteered often at the 700 Club. where he was in charge of and helped manage the counseling program. And every other day he was at the church counseling people for free.

Meanwhile, he had a daughter who suffered from spinal cancer. Charles invited me out to lunch one day. We went to Burger King and sat over at a table and talked about my teaching and other things. I had been teaching Bible studies back then.

At one point he said, "You don't mind if I pick up the tab for this, do you?" He pulled out a crisp new $100 bill to pay for the two hamburgers we ate. He said, "Don, people think that if you have money, you have it made. And it's amazing how people will come out of the woodwork to ask you flat out for money and this, that and the other. I don't give it to them all the time. If God speaks to me, I will give something to somebody, but somebody who shows up and just asks for money probably won't get it." And he said, "With all the money I have, and all the wealth that we enjoy, I would give it all in a heartbeat, if it could help my daughter with her spinal cancer, because money doesn't take care of everything."

Sometimes it takes us seeing someone in a position with money to realize money isn't everything. But for those who are in that position and don't realize it, they can also often become angry. Have you ever noticed that? Some rich people can be angry people, because they are used to getting their own way and have people fawn all over them. But the point is, "they have already received their comfort." That's a pretty powerful statement. Basically, Jesus is saying, "You have been resting in it. That's it. That's all you will get. There isn't any more."

"Woe to you who are well fed now for you will go hungry." Isn't that an interesting one? "Woe to you who laugh now! for you will mourn and weep." In Matthew Jesus says, "Blessed are they who mourn, for they will be comforted." It goes both ways. Here Jesus says, "Woe to you who laugh now, because you will mourn and weep."

What is it he's talking about here? He's talking about choices. It's nice to have wealth, I suppose. Not that I have had any to know firsthand. But I will tell you that having wealth isn't the end and isn't the answer. I have to make choices. If I won the lottery right now, I would like to think I would do all the right things with it.

I remember in my Senior Symposium in Business college class that I took to get my second degree; we calculated the worth of a lottery ticket. We figured out I how much people spend. The people who run the lottery actually get gazillions of times more money from people buying the tickets. What they give back is a drop in the bucket. The all-time record for a U.S. lottery drawing came in January 2016, when three winners split a prize of nearly $1.59 billion.

With the Publisher's Clearing House, although you pay for the stamp and they provide the envelope, for the odds of you winning, people way overspend what that stamp is worth. That's why people lick and mail another one and another one. Lick and stamp, lick and stamp. They mail them by the dozens to get rich. And the guys at Publisher's Clearing House rub their hands and laugh all the way to the bank. They found a cheap and easy way to make millions off of people. And along the way, perhaps some of those people will subscribe to some magazines. Theoretically, that's what it's all about. However, they never seem to have a magazine I want.

Anyway, those things don't work. They really don't. One or two people might win and that's great for them, but it's not a good way to think about providing for the future. You might get lucky, but it's extreme luck and nothing more. God may provide something like that, I don't know. But I often think if I won something, I would first want to get out of debt and have all these high-minded thoughts. I also know that if I can get that cool little thing I have been wanting, I am probably going to do that. And it doesn't take many of those before the amount you have dwindles. When money, or whatever it is, comes your way, you have already had your comfort. If that becomes what you rest on, be careful, because it won't last long. And it certainly won't last into the next life.

"Woe to you who are well fed now for you will go hungry." "Woe to you who laugh now for you will mourn and weep." "Woe to you when all men speak well of you, for that is how their fathers treated the false prophet." That's the second time he has pointed that out. When they speak well of you, watch out. When everybody thinks you are really cool, watch out. What exactly does that mean? "Woe to you when all men speak well of you." What is He saying here?

I asked this in a class I taught. One person said, "I think what He is getting at is that if you are going to listen to what people are saying, you need to differentiate between what you want to hear instead of what people tell you, or what you need to hear, they are different things."

Someone else said, "You know when everybody gives you a slap on the back and say, 'Yeah, good job man,' be careful. You might follow the crowd, or they could easily influence you. In that case you are following people instead of depending on Jesus."

So the problem occurs when you start to believe your own press. When everybody speaks well of you, you better start wondering what's going on. You better start paying attention because you may be missing something. I will guarantee you that. I mean, I love to teach and I like it when people thank me and say pleasant things about it. But if all I ever hear is how wonderful I am, I am going to wonder, *what's coming down the pike*? I love to play my horn. I like to hear from people when I play it well. But that's not the center of my universe. The center of my universe is not getting praise for what I do, whether it's teaching or playing music or whatever it is.

In a previous job, as a talented engineer, I had a meeting every other week. Basically 99.9% of the time, I do change requests for the firewall and I take incidents. A change request is when somebody needs something to go through a firewall in order to get something done. So they request the change and I work it through and make the change whereby they can test it. An incident is where something once worked, but then it broke. We call that a break fix. If it's a really serious incident, you know, because we usually hear about it. "You better hurry and get this incident fixed! There are millions of dollars pouring down the drain while you try to figure it out!"

I had literally cleaned up my entire list of 60 requests and incidents and whittled it down. In a meeting with my manager, I mentioned that to him, and he said, "What, how could you do that? My goodness!" I received some more changes, and I handled them, and I took some from some of the other guys' queues. It was nice to hear that they appreciated my work. But I had to be careful not to believe my own press, because suddenly I would point inward and become in danger of being in love with myself.

You must be careful of trusting in yourself and loving yourself. Don't say, "I am a self-made man and I love my creator."

"Woe to you who are rich, who are well fed now." "Woe to you when man speak well of you." "But I tell you who hear me, love your enemies, do good to those who hate you, bless those who curse you, pray for those who mistreat you. If someone strikes you on one cheek, turn to him the other as well. If someone takes your cloak, do not stop him from taking your tunic."

Do you know what led into this? Did you notice the woes preceding this advice he just gave us? Notice what connects the two. The first word in Verse 27 is "but." But is a redirecting conjunction. It is used to connect ideas that contrast. Let's see how many woes are there? There are only four woes, but that's still pretty important.

"But I tell you who hear me." Who is He telling? Whoever is listening. Not just those who can hear sound coming from His mouth, but those who hear Him. Listening is a volitional act. It is something you decide to do. You pay attention to the speaker. You decide to listen, hear, incorporate, and act on it. That's what hearing in this sense means.

But I tell you, who hear me, (here we go), "Love your enemies." "Do good to those who hate you," "Bless those who curse you," "Pray for those who mistreat you." That's hard. Lord, are you sure about this stuff?

But it gets worse. "If someone strikes you on the cheek, turn to him the other also." "If someone takes your cloak, do not stop him from taking your tunic." Isn't that interesting the way He does that? "Give to everyone who asks you and if anyone takes what belongs to you, do not demand it back." "Do to others as you would have them do to you."

We call that last statement the Golden Rule. It's amazing how many secular people appropriate that for themselves. Have you ever noticed what a high standard others expect of you when they know you consider yourself to be a Christian?

That's why people say, "I thought you said, you are a Christian. Aren't you supposed to always do this, that, or the other?" I mean, isn't it amazing how people who aren't Christians are aware of what Christians should do and how they are supposed to act, especially towards them? Isn't that amazing? Now it would be kind of cool if we really understood it as well as they did, or maybe even better. The difference is, it's even better if you not only understand it, but practice it, because stuff like with that Sergeant Major I mentioned earlier, doesn't happen in a vacuum. Those things happen when you practice it. Have you ever heard the expression, "Y'all pray for me, 'cause I need the prayer and y'all need the practice"?

We need to practice our belief. We need to practice these things Jesus tells us to do. He bundled them together and sort of wrapped up the other side, but hear Him, listen to what He has to say. "Love your enemies, do good to those who hate you." That's important and powerful when you do.

"Bless those who curse you." Bless means "happiness, happy, joyful," but bless those who curse you? What does that mean? How do you bless someone? Usually it's by doing something for them or giving them a monetary gift, or helping them out. Doing an unexpected good deed. Sometimes they may never hear you or see you do anything. Yet, you bless them to the throne of grace. That's when you say, "God bless that man, bless that woman, bless that person." That is a rich time in prayer.

There was a lady who came to me and she said, "You know I don't know what I did to this other woman. She seems to hate me. When we have the greeting time in church, she will look right through me and go right past me and shake somebody's else hand. What's that all about?"

I said, "I will tell you what. The best thing I can suggest you do is to pray for that woman regularly and God will put a love for her in your heart that you won't believe. He will. I promise."

She said, "Okay, I will do that." That was on a Thursday.

The following week during the midweek service on Wednesday, a young lady from the Bible College was playing and leading worship from the keyboard paused she paused and began weeping.

One guy in the congregation said, "Pastor, can I share a Scripture?" and I said, "Sure." He shared the Scripture found in Matthew 11:28-30, "Come to me, all you who are weary and burdened, and I will give you rest. Take my yoke upon you and learn from me, for I am gentle and humble in heart, and you will find rest for your souls. For my yoke is easy and my burden is light."

Then I got up and shared the passage in Matthew 5:23-24, "Therefore, if you are offering your gift at the altar and there remember that your brother has something against you, leave your gift there in front of the altar. First go and be reconciled to your brother; then come and offer your gift." I then mentioned Mark 11:25, "And when you stand praying, if you hold anything against anyone, forgive him, so that your Father in heaven may forgive you your sins." Finally, I said, "In either case, it's up to you to take the initiative." And as soon as I finished saying that, out of the corner of my eye, I saw this lady get up, walk across the back of the sanctuary, and kneel in front of that woman who visited me the previous week, and she asked her for forgiveness.

She said, "I don't know why, but I have had a hard time getting to like you. I just want forgiveness." It was a powerful moment and God was moving right there.

I am telling you, these things work. "Do good to those who hate you, bless those who curse you, pray for those who mistreat you." "If someone strikes you on one cheek, turn to him the other also." "Someone takes your cloak, do not stop him from taking your tunic." All that makes sense? See, this is meat and 'tater stuff. This is deep stuff from Christ and He is only getting started. This is early in his ministry. "Give to everyone who asks you and if anyone takes what belongs to you, do not demand it back." "Do to others as you would have them do to you." Then hear the balance that puts it in perspective. Jesus continued, "If you love those who love you, what credit is that to you? Even sinners love those who love them. And if you do good to those who are good to you, what credit is that to you? Even sinners do that. And if you lend to those from whom you expect repayment, what credit is that to you? Even sinners lend to sinners, expecting to be repaid in full."

Now it's okay to lend something to someone. But my suggestion is, don't lend something you are not willing to give and never see again. That's the attitude you need to have, not because, "They will probably never give it back, anyway." I'm saying in your heart, gift it to them. And if they bring it back, then it's a double blessing. In the interest of transparency, I have a stamp that I put in all of my important books which says, "From the Library of Rev. Donald F. Brown." I also make a note of it if I loan it to someone. However, since beginning that practice, I have never had to chase anyone down to recover my books.

"But love your enemies, do good to them." He is repeating himself in a way. "Lend to them without expecting to get anything back. Then your reward will be great and you will be sons of the Most High, because He is kind to the ungrateful and wicked. Be merciful just as your Father is merciful." Now that's an interesting note to end that section on, because grace is unmerited favor, but mercy is for somebody who deserves to be punished, but you choose not to punish. You bless instead.

Mercy is important, and that segues then into talking about judging. "Do not judge and you will not be judged." "Do not condemn and you will not be condemned." "Forgive and you will be forgiven." "Give and it will be given to you. A good measure, pressed down, shaken together and running over, will be poured into your lap. For the measure you use, it will be measured to you." Now that makes sense.

I was sitting in a church one time and they sang this song and it was something about the devil has to give you back a hundredfold for what he took from you or something like that. Ladies and gentlemen, I can't for the life of me find that in the Bible. Do you know where that is? Now it says that God will bless you, but we should not approach God or the things of God with expectation of undue, multiplied recompenses. Am I making sense here? There isn't a big predominance of the so-called prosperity teaching. But that's the thing they would teach. They rattled this song off, and then someone got up afterward and asked, "You believe that, right? You believe that? You believe it? Yes," and everybody whooped it up.

That I will get stuff back isn't the focus of my belief and worship. I am not in it for what I might get back. Here, Jesus said, "Don't be expecting anything back. Don't be looking for it back. If he takes one, let him take more, if he wants it."

"Give, and it will be given to you." And, "For with the measure you use, it will be measured to you." That's an interesting way to put it. And you know, if you find it, I would love to know about it. He also told them this parable.

Now let me tell you what a parable is first, before we go through it. A parable is a snapshot in words. It is a simple, easily understood picture in order to illustrate a point. It is not a major treatise of complicated theology on which to hang 10 pounds of meaning to every word in the parable. "And he said this and therefore it means that and then now, if it means that, it means something else."

You must be really careful with parables. Here is the parable. It's simple. "Can a blind man lead a blind man? Will they not both fall into a pit?" See how simple that is? A simple picture. If somebody who can't see is trying to lead somebody else who can't see, they are both liable to end up tripping into the pit. "A student is not above his teacher, but everyone who is fully trained will be like his teacher." "Why do you look at the speck of sawdust in your brother's eye and pay no attention to the plank in your own eye?" Wow, we have problems with that. We look at other people and say, "Didn't you see what he was doing the other day?" "Did you see so and so sleeping in church?"

"How can you say to your brother, brother, let me get the speck out of that eye, when you yourself fail to see the plank in your own eye? You hypocrite. First take the plank out of your eye, then you will see clearly to remove the speck from your brother's eye." Do you know how hard it is to see something clearly to accomplish a task, when your own problems blind you? And every one of us runs into something like this. It is dangerous and mutually destructive. You must be really careful about finding fault with everything.

"No good tree bears bad fruit, nor does a bad tree bear good fruit. Each tree is recognized by its own fruit. People do not pick figs from thorn bushes or grapes from briers. The good man brings good things out of the good stored up in his heart. And the evil man brings evil things out of the evil stored up in his heart. For out of the overflow of his heart, the mouth speaks." There is a big boom, right there. Jesus is not talking about stomach and fruit, he is talking about our innermost being. It's amazing how what's really in that innermost place manifests itself through what you say and how you address people. Jesus says, "you hypocrites." He used powerful language here. "Why do you call me Lord, Lord, and do not do what I say? I will show you what he is like who comes to me and hears my words and puts them into practice. He is like a man building a house who dug down deep and laid the foundation on a rock. When the flood came, the torrent struck that house, but could not shake it, because it was well built." Here is another one of those redirective conjunctions. "But the one who hears my words and does not put them into practice, is like a man who built a house on the ground without a foundation. The moment the torrent struck that house it collapsed and its destruction was complete."

Can you imagine going to all the trouble to build a house and you finally get it finished, but you built it on sand and when the first storm came along, it collapsed? What a total waste, a complete waste of effort.

Jesus has said these things before. He said, "If he hits you, strikes you on the cheek, turn your other cheek. If he steals from you, let him take your tunic too. Let him take your cloak and your tunic." But that's not being wimpy, nor being a pansy or whatever. It is being an agent of God's grace. Despite what the world says, there is no guarantee that there is an innate goodness about humans, because all have sinned and fallen short of God's glory. But often, circumstances reduce people to desperate acts, to take care of matters themselves. There is some of that out there, no doubt about it.

Some students from Central Bible College came down to the mission where I was working as a night chaplain. And this young student, all of eighteen years old, got up there to preach and he said, "When I was 17 years old, I went and did this and I did that and I got in trouble. My dad took away my driving privileges, so I have been where you are."

After the service we fed the guys who signed up to stay overnight and they got assigned bunks. Then they went out back to smoke and joke. One guy lit me up over what that young kid said.

He told me, "He does not know where I have been, he doesn't know my problems. He doesn't realize that I have a garage full of tools, 120 miles down the road. But I need to find a job and I can't find a job. I have to go where the work is. He does not know what I have been through. How dare this 17-year-old kid, who had his truck driving privileges and the pickup truck from daddy, say he knows where I have been and knows where I'm at?"

I ran into a lot of folks like that. They have to follow the work. Many of them work in construction because that's what's available, but they have to go where the construction is. They find out where it's going to be next and where they are hiring. They go from one job to the next to the next to the next to the next. That is a hard lifestyle. It can lead to all kinds of problems with self-esteem, etc. I know there are people out there who feel like they are in a corner and they have to provide for their family who might do a snatch and grab. They might steal something. Not everybody. Some people steal because they want to steal stuff and make a quick buck. But some people steal because they feel like they are out of alternatives.

I believe God will use you as an opportunity to bless someone when they take something and you let them take your tunic as well. That's what Jesus is talking about. That allows us to become an agent of grace in our own right, as provided by God through us to them. Is not everything we have part of His provision to us in the first place? Perhaps you see why it's not up to us to figure out which kind of thief someone is. God will deal with him or her, eventually, and if not before, He will certainly deal with in eternity. Hopefully, this person will have found Christ, but I am here to tell you these are the things Jesus practiced. And if you don't believe me, go watch "The Passion of the Christ," the Mel Gibson Production. If you have seen it, remember it. If you don't remember it, watch it again. Now there are some things in the movie that are a little over the top, but it perfectly depicts what Jesus is saying here.

I have been chipping away at a book I have always wanted to write called *Tenacious Grace*. Hopefully I will be able to complete it one of these days. The title came to me with the teardrop that fell down at the end of the movie and splashed on the ground at the foot of the cross. That blew me away: The tenacity Jesus had to exert to come to that point for you and me!

*Father, in Jesus' name, we are grateful to spend time together with your word, in your presence. Bless each one who has read this chapter. Bless us as we go to be a blessing to others as well. Let the words of Christ that we have looked at and dwelt on, find their way into our hearts and minds in an authentic way. We thank you Lord for all that you do, and we ask your blessing in Jesus' name. Amen.*

# Chapter 5

# I Am (Part 1)

*Father, in Jesus' name, we thank You, Lord, for all that you do in our lives. We pray, Lord, that You would speak to us. Let Your Word penetrate our hearts and get right to the core of our being with what Your son told us 2000 plus years ago. We thank you, Lord, for all that You do, and ask Your blessing in Jesus' name, Amen.*

In this chapter, we will delve into what Jesus had to say about Himself. It's interesting that these phrases, the "I Am" statements, are only in the Gospel of John. There are thirteen of them, but they are not anywhere else in the New Testament. None of the other Gospels have these. And each one of the thirteen describes a different aspect of who He is, as the Son of God and the Son of Man. We need to realize that language means a great deal.

We will begin with the first "I Am" statement. The writer scattered them throughout the Book of John. We will take them in Scripture order, the way He said them, and the order in which he recorded them. When does the Book of John begin? Look it up, if you don't know. It's a question with a point. And I might point at one of you for the answer.

The Gospel of John starts at the beginning. Why did He do that? There was an entire generation of people there. We already had three Gospels written by the time John writes his book. We believe the first one written was the Gospel of Mark, and the second one written was Matthew. Luke was not far behind that. And then John came along.

Mark was a young kid. He is the guy who was standing there, if you remember, when Jesus was being slapped around by the soldiers. Peter worried about it and Jesus told Peter, "Before the cock crows three times, you will disown me." Peter got accused not once, not twice, but three times. In Mark 14:51-52 we read, "A young man, wearing nothing but a linen garment, was following Jesus. When they seized him, he fled naked, leaving his garment behind." After Peter denied Jesus, someone saw this kid over there, and said, "He was with him, too," and Mark said, "No, I wasn't," and took off and somebody reached and grabbed him. He ran off and left his tunic there. We have the first streaker in the Bible. I don't know if you have heard that before or not. But most scholars assume that's Mark.

Mark was a young man in his mid to late teens, and he hung out with Peter. He followed Peter around and Peter discipled Mark. Mark's version of the Gospel read kind of like a Batman comic book. Do you remember those comic books and maybe even the TV series, "Batman"? Something would happen and the bad guy would come out and Batman would show up. He would punch a bad guy and "POW!" would fill the screen along with a loud blast of a musical chord. You read the Book of Mark and one thing after another happens. BOOM! this happens and POW! that happens, and ZAP! the Holy Spirit drove Him out into the wilderness to be tested. He fasted for 40 days, etc. A tumultuous series of events is recorded.

Matthew was a "bean counter." He's in accounting, like a CPA. They are precise and detail oriented. That was Matthew. He was a tax collector, but although he collected taxes for the Romans, he didn't like that job. Matthew is the one who lists all the different prophecies and Old Testament Scriptures that were fulfilled by various things Jesus said and did. He had a different take on things. He was Jewish and when Jesus spoke to him, he dropped what he was doing and came along to follow Jesus.

Then there was Luke, who Paul discipled as he accompanied him on his missionary journeys. Now if you read the Book of Luke, the same guy wrote it who wrote the Book of Acts. The first part of the Book of Acts through about the first half of Chapter 9, Luke wrote in the third person, "They did this, and they went there and someone stopped them," and so on. Then suddenly about halfway through chapter 9, Luke began writing in the first person plural, "We went here, and we went there and an angel stopped us." He shifts from third person to first person plural because at that point Luke was there with Paul for the remainder of the book.

He accompanied Paul, and he heard and learned what he wrote from Paul, which became his Gospel and the first part of Acts. Luke was a physician. Physicians do what they do with great compassion for people. That comes through in Luke's writing. When we read these different things. you understand that about the authors of each of these three books. All by itself, that can tell you a great deal about what's being said.

People want to quibble about, "Well, it says something here, and it's different over there, so that's wrong. I mean, you know, the Bible it's got problems you know." Well, I don't know any such thing. The apparent discrepancies simply mean it's written by different people from different perspectives and different points of view. And that's important to understand because Jesus did things from two points of view as well. Do you know what they were? The two points of view are the Son of God and the Son of Man. Many things Jesus said or did were as the Son of Man. A lot of the things He said or did were as the Son of God. When He stood up that day in the Sanhedrin and read from the Book of Isaiah, that was the Son of God speaking when, at the end of the passage in Isaiah, He said, "This is fulfilled in your hearing this day."

We have two Jewish people and one gentile physician, who had written the first three Gospels. The gentile got all his stuff in his Gospel from Paul, who was a bright, young theological scholar, a rising star in the Sanhedrin. Those three books have a Jewish angle to them.

John was the beloved disciple. That's how he refers to himself in the third person throughout the Gospel of John. But John is the one who the Roman Emperor Titus Flavius Domitianus exiled to the Isle of Patmos. The Romans wanted to squash this horrible new religion, because people went to it in droves. They flocked to this new thing. The Romans didn't like that a bit, because it ate away at their power. The Pharisees and Sadducees didn't like it a bit either, because it took away from their power. There was a great deal of animosity that ebbed and flowed back and forth then.

When the time came, they lay siege to Jerusalem. Christians and the rest of the population starved and ate things and did things that were unmentionable. They were under the heel of the Roman Empire. Therefore, John found himself exiled. And in this complete sequestration, out by himself on this desert island with the bare minimum to eat or drink to stay alive, is where God spoke to him. That's when we get the Revelation, and there is only one by the way. The first line says, "The revelation of Jesus Christ." It's the Revelation of the one and only Jesus Christ to John, not the Revelations as some call it by mistake.

Finally, he gains release from the Isle of Patmos. We don't have details on how, but we know enough about when. Because he later became the Pastor Emeritus of the Church in Ephesus. Paul is the one who planted the Church in Ephesus. Do you remember the Book of Ephesians and the Book of First Timothy? They were respectively a letter to the church at Ephesus, and a letter to Timothy, who Paul left behind to oversee the Ephesian Church. And then he wrote a second letter to Timothy, although

Timothy was somewhere else by then. Paul, in the meantime, had been in prison once, and was in prison a second time. I don't know if you have seen the movie "Paul, Apostle of Christ." It is about the time in Paul's life when he was in jail a second time. We find the second imprisonment in Second Timothy. But the last imprisonment we find in the Book of Acts, Chapter 28, ends Paul's imprisonment. The second imprisonment reflected in Second Timothy is not recorded anywhere else.

Paul wrote several epistles from prison. The first time, the court of Caesar imprisoned him. There, they treated him pretty well. But times had changed and the second imprisonment took place around the time of Nero, the fifth Roman emperor. The time span was pretty large.

When John came back from Patmos to Ephesus, he wrote this fourth Gospel. He started at the beginning, "(En arkhê êin ho Logos) In beginning was the word, (kai ho logos êin pros tòn theón) and the word was toward/with the God, (kai theós êin ho Logos) and God was the word."

That's John 1:1 in transliterated Greek. "In the beginning was the Word, and the Word was with God, and the Word was God." It translates literally. If you have heard of archaeology, En arkhêi, in the beginning, archaeology is the study of first things. And eschatos, last things, gives us the study of last things, eschatology. It refers to the end of the universe, and it also refers to what happens after we die. So in the beginning was the Word, translated from the Greek, Logos, the Word, not any old word. Logos in the New Testament always refers to the written word.

There is another word and you may or may not have run across, Rhema. Rhema is often also translated as word, but it can refer either to the written word or to a spoken word. To give you an example of the difference, Jesus taught along the shore, which was a sort of natural amphitheater. He preached and when He finished, He turned around and told the guys to cast their nets.

When they said, "Lord, we have been out here all day, there is nothing out here, we will catch nothing." I mean, He had been teaching the Word, the Logos all day long, but "nevertheless at your word, (they used the word Rhema there), we will do it." They cast their nets and they could barely pull them in and the nets were breaking. The ships almost sank. He taught the Word, and they said, "nevertheless at your word, (Rhema) we will do what you say. That's a good example of the difference between the two. Rhema doesn't always refer to one or the other, but Logos always refers to the written word.

When we see that, then we begin in the beginning. Well, that's kind of weird, because the Word wasn't in written form yet. Now we understand that when we say Jesus is the living Word, it's real. In Hebrews 1:3, it says Jesus is the exact representation of the Heavenly Father. "The Son is the radiance of God's glory and the exact representation of his being, sustaining all things by his powerful word. After he had provided purification for sins, he sat down at the right hand of the Majesty in heaven." Jesus is the exact representation of the Father. If you think about that for a moment, when Jesus comes into the world, it was a sort of shock for Mary to know that she would conceive a child and His name would be Emmanuel. That struck her as weird. She was fearful when she heard the angel say what he said.

As this child grew in favor with God and man, we saw a young man who had stepped aside from the so-called Adamic bloodline, and introduced by the Holy Spirit, into the human race. There is a lot to be said about soteriology and all these things that talk about salvation and what they mean. But Jesus, being the exact representation of God, looks at more than what He looks like or His height. His earthly father was a carpenter, and He grew up as a carpenter's son. He was strong, had rough hands like a carpenter, because they didn't have cool tools in those days. You had to work the hard way with a hammer and whatever else it took to do carpentry. Then Jesus entered ministry. His mom "pondered these things in her heart." What an amazing little 13 to 16-year-old girl. It would scare most kids to death in our culture today. They wouldn't know what to do. They would talk about the latest gossip while popping bubblegum and being cool or whatever. But Mary treasured these things in her heart. It was no surprise to her when Jesus was ready to enter into ministry.

So we started reading in the beginning was the word, the word was with God and the word was God. And in Verse 14, "The word became flesh and dwelt among us. And we beheld His glory as the only Begotten Son of God." Then we reach the end of Chapter 1, and there they are, in the Second Chapter of John at the Wedding Feast of Cana, where they ran out of wine. Mary said to the servants, "Do whatever he tells you." At Mary's behest, Jesus told the servants, "Go get some water." Really. They took it to the guy in charge, who tasted it, and was astounded, because he said, "Normally people serve their best wine first, and save the worst wine for last." They get you started on the good stuff, then rotgut when you can't tell the difference, because they don't want to waste it. "But this is by far the best wine we have had all day."

Was it an alcoholic wine or was it plain old grape juice? I don't care because it doesn't matter for our purposes. That's not the point. My guess is, it was most likely alcohol. They didn't know the difference back then. And they didn't guzzle it all day. They drank it as a normal part of the social intercourse of life. For them, it wasn't a big deal. And it shouldn't be to us. We can get wrapped around the axle sometimes about the dumbest things.

But if you think about it, once it goes through the fermentation process and it turns into wine over a long time, making it quite safe to drink. Germs will not grow in it, because there's alcohol in there. Have you ever heard of places where people say, "If you go, don't drink the water?" I have been there, I tried that.

We went out to Yuma, Arizona, once and on the way back I was thirsty. I drank out of the water fountain at one of the rest stops and boy, that was a mistake! I paid for that for two days. Who knows what's in those pipes? But that doesn't happen with wine. Wine is not susceptible to that. The amoebas or whatever is in water can't survive there. They didn't know that, but God did.

Paul says at one point, "a little wine is good for the stomach." But back to the actual point, in the second chapter of John, Jesus has just started His earthy ministry, and the writer records the first miracle of Jesus right there. It's the only Gospel which records this miracle where He turned water into wine. There are seven miracles in the Book of John. Each one is different. This one demonstrates His mastery as God over matter. He turns water into wine.

Then midway through the chapter, we jump ahead to the last two weeks of Jesus' earthly life. We leap ahead from the Marriage Feast of Cana, to what we often refer to as the Passion of the Christ and the events that immediately precede it. Everything said and done from there on, in the Book of John, is all from the last two weeks of His earthly life. Did you know that?

Stop and think about how significant this is. John wrote with a purpose. He had a specific message that he wanted to give to people who were not familiar with the Jewish culture. Maybe they didn't grow up in Israel all their lives. Luke hadn't. He was a gentile, but he hung with Paul, therefore, he got a pretty good handle on that part of it. But John felt it necessary to go back to the beginning and explain things so people could understand what this Jesus phenomenon was all about. John was a pretty bright man.

Let me give another aside. Luke may be the second most intellectual guy of the New Testament writers. Paul is, by a pretty respectful distance, the most intellectually capable person of the writers of the New Testament books. I have translated some of

Paul's writing and John's writing and some others from Greek into English and I will tell you, Paul is much more complex. Luke is pretty complex himself. Mark is somewhat simple; he was just a kid. John is some simple too, but he was straightforward in his language, he didn't pull any punches. Paul was a master craftsman with language, and the words he chose would always be the exact right ones to say what he had to say. As Jesus did not actually write anything of which we are aware, we must rely on the Gospel accounts to convey what He said. Of those, John sets himself apart as capturing a completely unique segment of the things Jesus said in a way that gives a very insightful understand of who Jesus the Son of Man and the Son of God truly was.

My goal is to excavate stuff that you haven't heard before. I want to do it in a way that captures it and can transform your understanding of the New Testament and the word. In Jesus' day, they only had the Old Testament. We can go back and read John and what he had to say, and we can hear the advice of Jesus through John. We can go back and read the Pauline Epistles and all these things. But they didn't have that available to them. You know why? They were living it and by their life, they were writing it. What we are doing, the fabric of life, is the fabric of language and interaction between people. That's what we are seeking to achieve with the "Jesus Said What?" theme. I hope you will see the interactions and the depth and power of language used under the influence of the Holy Spirit in this written Word we call the New Testament. It is astounding how God weaves this together.

There was a guy who was a Russian mathematician. Russians are wizards with math and chess. This mathematician sought to show the fallacy of the Bible. He started from Genesis 1:1 all the way to Revelation 22:21 to find every numeric relationship and prove that the Bible is full of baloney. He could not find a single mathematical construct, concept, or relationship, with a flaw, or a flawed relationship to other things. And he came to Christ as a result.

He was like a mathematical C.S. Lewis, who did the same thing. Lewis went on a journey and you know who led him to the Lord? J.R.R. Tolkien. They were buddies, and they both taught at Cambridge University. When we talk about language, we talk about something that is the lifeblood of relationships. How good a relationship do you have, if nobody ever talks to anybody? I guess you would have a pretty highly developed sign language or something, I suppose. But how do you not communicate?

In John Chapter 6:35, Jesus declared, "I am." Let's talk about what happens before and after the context. There are two Greek words, ego, pronounced egg-ō, and eimi, pronounced ay-mee. Now the first of those, ego, is that from which we get the modern word "ego." Somebody is a real egotist. An egotistical person is all about him or herself. In psychology, people talk about the id and the ego. They say the id is the lower self. The id is the part that says, "me hungry." The ego says, "I want caviar." We get the word ego, which in psychology refers to the higher self. These are the Greek words they came from. The second word, eimi, is part of the basic verb that's in every earthly language of which we know, the verb "to be." The root is "es" which means be, and adding the suffix "mi" to form "eimi" converts the verb to first person singular meaning, "I am." Shakespeare said, "to be or not to be, that is the question." Anyway, "to be" first person singular is "I Am." Now He repeats Himself or so it would seem, because ego is self-reference and eimi is I Am. First person verb, singular, ego, eimi, I Am. In effect, the phrase means literally, "I, I am."

Here's something else about these two little Greek words. There were about 70 scholars who were in Alexandria, Egypt. Now the City of Alexandria got its name from its conqueror, Alexander, the Great. When Alexander conquered all the known world, he named everything after himself. Alexander was from this little island called Helios. It was part of the larger group of islands belonging to Greece. He had a desire to have a legacy of conquering all the people and lands, and he wanted them to remain under the control of his descendants. One thing he did to accomplish that was what we refer to today as Hellenization from the Isle of Helios. He imposed their culture from Helios upon the culture of the peoples they conquered. He taught them how to speak and to write Greek. Greek became the language of commerce, and people would write letters, etc. Alexander had pesky Jews hanging around. The 70 scholars, at the behest of Alexander the Great, sat down and translated the entire Old Testament into Greek. We know it today as the Septuagint from the Septa in Latin, which means 70.

They translated the 39 books of the Old Testament into Greek as they used it in the time of Alexander the Great. In about 600 AD, a Catholic scholar called St. Jerome came along and decided he would do everybody a favor. He got the Septuagint and translated it and the New Testament from Greek, the original language of the New Testament, into Latin. That became known as the Latin Vulgate. However, he didn't understand that there were a bunch of books that weren't part of the Scriptures. We know those today as the Apocrypha. The Catholic Bible has the Old Testament, the Apocrypha, and the New Testament. Apocrypha means away from or out of, and therefore, they are not part of the Bible. But because St. Jerome translated them into Latin, the Catholic Church adopted his Latin translation.

They included the Apocrypha as part of the official Catholic Bible. In that day and age, and later when Jesus came along, many people saw the Apocrypha kind of like we see Christian fiction today. Remember the *Left Behind Series?* A few years ago, the *Left Behind Series* was very popular and many in Christian circles read them, but that's not Scripture. I mean, it's a consistent take from the point of view of the authors. And it's pretty faithful to its version of interpreting the information we have from Revelation. But it's not to be taken as Scripture, and I don't think many people would read it the same way as the Bible. And they never said that about any of the books in the Apocrypha back then. But because Jerome was without understanding, he included it, and it then became part of the Catholic Bible. I am sure you have laid awake at night, worrying about that.

That's why the Catholic Bibles are the only ones who continue to use it today. King James was a Protestant king, and he sponsored the new translation from the original Greek in the New Testament and the original Hebrew. They didn't use or refer to the Latin Vulgate. They went right back to original sources in Hebrew for the Old Testament and Greek for the New Testament.

In the Bible, Moses wandered around up there on the mountain. He looked to the side and saw a bush that was burning without being consumed. There wasn't any smoke or anything like that coming from it. Moses tiptoed a little closer and heard a voice that said, "Moses, take off your shoes; you are standing on holy ground."

During the conversation Moses was having with God, who is working with him through the burning bush experience, we find in Exodus 3:13 Moses said to God, "Suppose I go to the Israelites and say to them, 'The God of your fathers has sent me to you,' and they ask me, 'What is his name?' Then what shall I tell them?" God said to Moses, "I Am Who I Am. This is what you are to say to the Israelites: 'I Am has sent me to you.'" Guess how they translated I Am into the Septuagint Greek: Egō eimi, "I, I Am."

Let me tell you something about the Observant Jews. I don't know how observant they are, if they did the whole thing with the payot or anything else, but Observant Jews will avoid saying the name of God. They always talk about God in the third person. "May He, who causes the flowers to bloom, bless you." They won't say, "May God bless you," because they are afraid of saying the name of God wrong, or in vain. They do not want to bring judgment on themselves by profaning or blaspheming His name.

That's why Observant Jews will never say God or they will never say His name. You need to understand that because everything we talk about now hinges on understanding that.

God sent Moses, and He said, "When you get there, tell them, 'I Am that I Am, the I Am has sent you.'" And they translated that little two-word phrase, the self-reference pronoun 'I' and then the first person singular verb 'I Am.' What does Moses do? Now think about it from a linguistic standpoint. I Am. And if you stop and think about that simple phrase, God is trying to express in terms that Moses could comprehend His eternal self-existence. You might want to write that down, because that's some deep stuff. I Am, in those two simple words express God in His eternal self-existence.

In John 6:35, Jesus declared "ego eimi the bread of life." "I, I am the bread of life." Every time He used that phrase, 13 times recorded in the Book of John, if the Jews heard Him, they cringed. They considered it blasphemy to say the name of God. Jesus said it freely. He didn't pull any punches when He said, "I am the bread of life." He came out and said that stuff. And the Sadducees and Pharisees would never do that.

Do you remember reading about when Jesus stood up in the Synagogue to read the Book of Isaiah that we referred to earlier? Some people were angry. But some people said, "Wow, this guy doesn't speak like the scribes and the Pharisees. This guy speaks like He knows what it is. He speaks with authority. He talks and it comes into existence." Okay, maybe they didn't say all of that, but they something was different about Jesus.

In the first one He says, "I am the bread of life." I don't know how much you know about the sixth chapter of John. Have you read the Bible through, straight through, or in some semblance on a regular basis? If you don't, you should. I will tell you that every time you read it, you will read the same stuff, with simple things over and over, and see additional things every time. God speaks to you every single time. The Holy Spirit draws you into the word every single time and draws His word out of you every single time. This is a lifelong process.

Let's go on a little adventure, "I am the bread of life." Now what happened? Those folks followed Him around. In verse 6:28 they ask, "What must we do to do the works God requires of us?" Jesus replied, "The work of God is this, believe in the one he has sent." They said, "What miraculous sign will you give that we may see it and believe in you? What will you do? Our forefathers ate manna in the desert as it is written, he gave them bread from heaven to eat."

If you go back to verse 25, they asked, "Hey, when did you get here?" and He said, "I will tell you the truth, you are looking for me, not because you saw miraculous signs, but because you ate the loaves and had your fill. Don't work for food that spoils but for food that endures to eternal life, which the Son of Man will give you. On him, God the Father has placed his seal of approval. Then they asked, what are we supposed to do that we would do the works of God? He said, the work of God is this, believe in the one he has sent. And then they said, "what miraculous sign will you give us?" If it were me, I would think, you idiot, you just had a miraculous sign. Your bellies are full, I just told you that. But anyway, He didn't. He was polite. It's a good thing I'm not Jesus. He said, "I will tell you the truth, it is not Moses who has given you the bread from heaven, but it is My Father who gives you the true bread from heaven. For the bread of God is He who comes down from heaven and gives life to the world." "Sir, they said from now on give us this bread." And here it comes, "Ego eimi, I am the bread of life. He who comes to me will never go hungry, and he who believes in me will never be thirsty."

The Jews grumbled, and Jesus admonished them to stop grumbling among themselves. In verse 44, Jesus said, "No one comes to me, unless the Father who sent him, draws him: and

I will raise him up at the last day." In verse 45 He said, "It is written in the Prophets, they will be all taught by God, everyone who listens to the Father and learns from him, comes to me, no one has seen the Father except the one who is from God. Only he has seen the Father, I will tell you the truth. He who believes has everlasting life. I am the Bread of Life." There is that phrase again. "Your forefathers ate manna in the desert, yet they died. But here is the bread that comes down from heaven, which a man may eat and not die. I am the living bread that came down from heaven. If anyone eats up this bread, he will live forever." There is that promise again. It's the third time if anybody wants to keep count.

In verse 53, He tells them, "'I will tell you that unless you eat the flesh, of the Son of Man and drink his blood, you have no life in you, whoever eats my flesh and drinks my blood, has eternal life and I will raise him up at the last day, for my flesh is real food, and my blood is real drink. Whoever eats my flesh and drinks my blood, remains in me and I and him. Just as the Father sent me and I live because of the Father. So the one who feeds on me will live because of me, this is the bread that came down from heaven. Your forefathers ate manna and died. But he who feeds on this bread will live forever.' He said this while still teaching in the synagogue in Capernaum. Hearing this, many of the disciples said, this is a hard teaching. Who can accept it?"

Can you imagine? They are being told to eat this guy. Is it cannibalism or what? This is weird, Jesus. Or that's unclean or something. I mean, who knows what was going through their minds, but their brains exploded. So this is one of those moments, Jesus said What? Now let's walk back.

He gives His promise several times. In verse 39 we read, "And this is the will of him who sent me, that I shall lose none of all that he has given me, but raise them up at the last day." Being raised up in the last day is the promise. In verse 40, "For my Father's will is that everyone who looks to the Son and believes in him shall have eternal life, and I will raise him up at the last day." That's a two piece promise: Shall have eternal life, AND I will raise him up at the last day.

And then 44 says, "No one can come to me unless the Father who sent me draws him, and I will raise him up at the last day." This single promise also repeats. Here is another single promise.

> "I tell you the truth, he who believes has everlasting life. I am the bread of life. Your forefathers ate the manna in the desert, yet they died. But here is the bread that comes down from heaven, which a man may eat and not die. I am the living bread that came down from heaven. If anyone eats of this bread, he will live forever. This bread is my flesh, which I will give for the life of the world" (John 6:47-51, NIV).

He will live forever. Now, we see a third repeat of this promise here. "Whoever eats my flesh and drinks my blood has eternal life, and I will raise him up at the last day." (John 6:54) Again you see the two piece promise.

Some promises, like eternal life and raised up at the last day, go together. Some of them only have part of that. How do we sort this out? What does this mean? Are we supposed to go and eat this guy, and if so, unless He multiplies Himself like He did the fishes and the loaves, we are stuck. We end up with nothing left to eat. I would hope it doesn't mean that in the literal sense. And yet, I don't think that the folks who are listening to Him quite made that distinction. I don't think the distinction came about until later. There was a great deal of what Jesus said and did that they did not comprehend. Even those who were with Him for the entire three-year earthly ministry didn't get it until after they crucified Him, and then reappeared after He resurrected from the dead. And only then did they understand. Remember the two guys on the Road to Emmaus in Luke 24:30–31? "When he was at the table with them, he took bread, gave thanks, broke it and began to give it to them. Then their eyes were opened and they recognized him, and he disappeared from their sight." Ding, the light came on.

Let's go back, instead of forward, to understand this. Look at Verse 35, "I am the bread of life," is where the first statement came about, "Egō, eimi the bread of life. He who comes to me, will never go hungry." Who is taking action? We are coming to Him, and the result is that we never go hungry. "He who believes in me…." Who is taking action? We are believing in Him, and the result is that we will never be thirsty. "So eat my flesh, drink my blood, come to me, never hunger, believe in me, never thirst." This is a careful use of language and it is consistent for this entire session. You get that? You see it? This is good stuff!

We come to Christ and believe Him and never hunger, eat His flesh, and never thirst, drink His blood. When we approach Him, you take the initiative, you decide, you come to Christ. Then you lay everything down, trust Him, and believe in Him. That's where He takes care of thirst. That's where the blood comes in. What do we do during communion? We sip a little bit of grape juice, which symbolizes the blood of Jesus.

Have you ever been in a military chapel during communion, by the way? If someone invites you and if you don't want to be caught drinking actual alcoholic wine, when it comes around, take the purple grape juice on the outside few rings. They will have some in the middle, that is white, and that is actual alcoholic wine.

We use white grape juice at my church, but military chapels have a lot of folks from a lot of different backgrounds. They have some who follow one tradition, and some who are used to another. They put the white, alcoholic wine in the middle and then non-alcoholic grape juice on the outside and it is purple. Just so you know, that was some free advice.

Some have asked about the teachings of Calvinism as it relates to this subject. My brother and his wife are outgoing with their faith. They lived near my mom. My mother married a guy, my step-father, who was an agnostic. I don't know whether he ever came to Christ before he died. It wouldn't surprise me if he didn't, it would be a tremendous moment of celebration if I find out he did. But my brother and his wife, when they had the opportunity, would try to share Christ with him.

Some people believe in predestination, but the biggie is election. Romans 8:29-30 states, "For those God foreknew he also predestined to be conformed to the likeness of his Son, that he might be the firstborn among many brothers. And those he predestined, he also called; those he called, he also justified; those he justified, he also glorified."

Paul, in Ephesians, talks a lot about predestination. But predestination as I understand it from Scripture, and that's the entire council of Scripture, not just proof text here and there, comes from foreknowledge. Now let me unpack that a little. One objection to election is that if it's up to my free will to choose God, then that somehow is a problem for God's sovereignty. Believe it or not, they say that for us to have free will would somehow diminish Gods sovereignty. So the Calvinist view is that we are elect and God in His sovereignty chooses who goes to heaven. But the problem with that is, he has already decided ahead of time, who is going to go to heaven and who can't, so it doesn't matter what choices you make now, does it? And then they say, "No, no, what you want to do is strive to become the best Christian you can, if you are part of the elect, and if you aren't, you know you are not."

It's a tough concept to defend because the way I see God is way bigger than my imagination can conjure up. He is way beyond anything I can conceive. In terms of His immensity, it is limitless. In terms of His knowledge, it is unfathomable.

God is immense, amazing, and complex. He created us in His image, but we are far from being equal to Him. Yet every part of us, not just what we look like, but our faculties, our personalities, reflects His image. Human beings are creative beings. Did you know that? If you don't, look around. How many books and pieces of music and all kinds of creative expression can you think of, and you never hear the same thing twice after thousands of years of making music, and writing words, and making poetry?

In God's amazing size and immensity and love for you and I, God is so big that it doesn't matter how terribly I act, or how many times I screw up. I can do the stupidest stuff and still not break down His sovereignty, because He can make room in His plan for me to be an idiot. And it won't faze him a bit. There is another thing that goes along with this, and maybe this will help convey the idea.

Envisage a great ferocious warfare, with the devils all over one side and God over on the other side. Luke 11:19 states, "Now if I drive out demons by Beelzebub, by whom do your followers drive them out? So then, they will be your judges." God says it is not the power of anything else above that did it, but it's the power of the Holy Spirit. In Luke 11:20, God says, "But if I drive out demons by the finger of God, then the kingdom of God has come to you." God's not in a sweat. He doesn't worry about the devil and He hasn't time at all for you. He has nothing but eternity!

This is big stuff. We need to understand what an immense God we serve. "Those whom he foreknew, he predestined for his glory." Because of His fore knowledge, He already knew I was going to do something stupid. He sort of made a little downsized idiot hole for me, to be stupid and still not worry about breaking His sovereignty. That's how I see this whole thing. When John

Calvin came along and said all this stuff about election and predestination and so forth, another guy named Arminius came along and said, "Wait a minute, hold it. How can you say all of this stuff and obliterate our free will?" God created us as free agents, with the ability to choose.

There is a pretty good picture in the Revelation. The dragon appears before the woman. He sweeps his tail and a third of the stars of heaven fall. The stars represent angels. The good news is the angels who fell are outnumbered two to one! Anyway, that's how we know, but there are other places, too, I suppose, but that's the one I like the best. It's the coolest. It's the Batman comic book.

Martin Luther began with the idea of predestination and he didn't like the book of James, because the book of James plays havoc with this idea of election that Luther broached. He referred to the book of James as "a right strawy little epistle." He didn't like it much because there is stuff in there that flies against his idea of election. That's the thing, the entire council of God doesn't support that doctrine, in my opinion. When you look at it, and read it, you realize these other guys, the Arminians, came along and said, "We have free will and that doesn't affect God's sovereignty." He created us that way on purpose. He also has angels and they help implement His will. Those who didn't got swept out of heaven to hell.

Do you think the devil can get saved ever? Why not? You are pretty sure he can't, but why not? It goes back to Genesis, all the way back. A murder mystery unfolds. The serpent lay in wait for Adam and Eve to walk by him on their morning walk. He didn't even talk to Adam and Adam doesn't even care to engage him in conversation. The serpent talks to Eve.

And he said, "Did God really say, 'You must not eat from any tree in the garden?'" The first thing the devil does, is try to get Eve to doubt God. He doesn't lie and say, "God doesn't tell the truth," he just said, "Did God really say?"

And she said, "God did say, 'You must not eat fruit from the tree that is in the middle of the garden, and you must not touch it, or you will die.'"

"You will not surely die," the serpent said to the woman. "For God knows that when you eat of it, your eyes will be opened, and you will be like God, knowing good and evil."

When the woman saw that the fruit of the tree was good for food and pleasing to the eye, and also desirable for gaining wisdom, she took some and ate it. She also gave some to her husband, who was with her, and he ate it. (Genesis 3:1-6, NIV)

The devil didn't come out and lie to them. They made a choice of free will, but then the next thing you know, God showed up in the cool of the morning and said, "Hey, Adam, Eve! Where are you guys?"

Adam relied, "We were hiding here in the bushes, because we are naked."

God asked, "Who told you that you were naked?" Adam immediately blamed it on Eve saying, "This woman you gave me over here."

God then asked Eve, "Who told you, you were naked?"

Eve passed the buck to the serpent, "Well, this serpent over here," and God didn't even ask the serpent.

God said, "Her offspring's heel will crush your head and you will strike his heel." Her seed. That's the first time the Bible foretells Jesus in the Bible, right there in Garden as recorded in the Book of Genesis.

Here is the murder mystery I told you about. The fruit looked good to eat, "Mm! Me hungry!" Remember that body and flesh? It's beautiful, that's our artistic sense. I am an artist and when I see good art, it's all subjective. Some people think it's ugly. But it's a head thing. It's good to make me like God. There's my ego. Of those things, does the serpent feed or even pretend to feed your spiritual self? It deals with your soul, which includes your intellect and ego, and your body. These two conspire together to eliminate the influence of the spirit and do what this serpent suggested they do, because that fruit is there and it's big and real.

That day a murder took place. The human spirit was the victim of a homicide. Today, we talk about two things that take place and we talk about it two ways. Jesus saves us and we are born again. Now do you get what's happening here? Every one of us deserves death for our sin, that is the penalty for sin. He saves us from that penalty. But He also brings us back to life. The Holy Spirit grabs hold of your innermost being, your spirit, and draws him back to life, and you are born again, a brand-new creation in Christ.

What's the first thing God does? He starts a conversation. Did you know God talked to Himself? At the beginning part of it, he says, "Hmm, let us create, let us make man, let us make man and woman in our image, man and woman he made them." And then later he has another conversation that goes something like this. "We have got to get these guys out of here. Now that they have eaten from the tree of knowledge of good and evil, we must remove them from the garden so that they cannot eat of the tree of life, and become like us, and live forever." Kicking them out of the garden was not punishment, it paved the way for salvation. The angels could not die, they were already eternal beings. Therefore, the devil, even if he wanted to, could never be saved, because no one can die in his place. We alone have that highest calling and privilege in all of God's creation. Jesus gave His life for US!

We must understand how big God's love is. This is meat and potatoes, folks. It astonishes me every time I think about it.

The second "I Am," statement is John 8:12: "When Jesus spoke again to the people, he said, 'ego eimi, I am the light of the world. Whoever follows me will never walk in darkness, but will have the light of life.'"

They wanted to see God, and that's a problem. What do you think is going on in the Middle East right now? With ISIS and the so-called caliphate. They believe that their movement will be the precursor for Mohammad's successor.

It was about the 7th century when Muhammad showed up and introduced and developed his Muslim doctrine. He would say things and someone would write it down, because he was illiterate, he couldn't read or write. It became the Quran, after a while. Muslims base their holy book on all the things he said. The God of Islam, however, is not the same as the God in the Bible. He is not, nowhere near, not even close.

But the real God, when we talked about the Beatitudes, that's why the Beatitudes work the way they do. If you want to be God or replace the real God, you will not do anything found in the Beatitudes. You will essentially say, "I Am God, I am in charge." And what happens? Every time a government, people, or group comes and takes over and they throw God out, they become totalitarian. And what do totalitarian regimes do? Atheistic regimes have no moral compass, cause or recourse. Anytime they tell people this is the right way to live, behave, or to think, they can only command it by fiat, and implement it by force. That's why socialism will always destroy and never build up. There has never been a case of successful socialistic thinking and governance that would last more than a generation or two, maybe three. For example, China has been hanging on pretty good, but that is a mess over there. China has an amazing history, but the advent of Communist rule has destroyed all of that.

For people without God, there is no recourse and they can only force their will by fiat, alright. In John 8:12, when God spoke again to the people, He said, "Ego eimi, I am the light of the world, whoever follows me will never walk in darkness, but will have the light of life." In Proverbs 119:95 we read, "Thy word is a lamp unto my feet, and a light unto my path." Why not thy word is a lamp unto my shoulder or my belly or my head or something like that? Why do you think only feet? How much illumination does God give you from His word? Enough for the next step. He doesn't tell you the entire journey.

They say, "A journey of a thousand miles begins with one step," but "Thy word is a lamp unto my feet," means His word will be there to guide you and to give you light for every step throughout your life. "I am the light of the world" is beyond the word thing for the feet since Jesus is the Word according to John 1:1. He is the illumination of life anywhere and everywhere throughout the planet.

Now how is light defined and how is darkness defined? How do we define darkness? Sometimes it is bad or evil. How else do we define darkness? Think like a physicist for a minute. One is we cannot see. Why not? Because it's dark, and also because of blindness. Darkness is an absence of light. Light is not an absence of darkness. Light will always fill up a space. This tiniest light will light up a room. I can turn on my phone and from its glow, I don't have to turn any lights on and wake up my wife when I am getting up early to go to work. I use the glow and that's enough. It doesn't take much light for me to see how to get around.

When Jesus says He is the light of the world, that's pretty astonishing. What kind of light are we talking about? We are not talking about light bulbs. When we talk about the world, who are we talking about? "Whoever follows me will never walk in darkness, but will have the light of life." He gave us a description there. It is following Him. And that has to do with the process of life. You can follow anybody or you can follow nothing but if you follow Him, whoever follows Him will never walk in darkness. If it's getting kind of dark where you are, then maybe you didn't take a left when He did.

Think about it, if you are far from Jesus, then who turned? Who wasn't paying attention? Anyway, light has an internal quality and an eternal quality to it. And I would submit, an infinite quality to it. All the things that are true of God are true of His being the light of the world. He fills the world with light. Anyway, God is He who casts no shadow when He turns around. James 1:17 states, "Every good gift and every perfect gift is from above, and cometh down from the Father of lights, with whom is no variableness, neither shadow of turning." Have you ever read that? That's an amazing picture. Can you imagine that? And yet, all things confronted with him and His light cast a shadow. They are opaque. He is translucent. He emanates light and there is no darkness in Him and he casts no shadow in turning. Jesus says, "Ego eimi, the light of the world, and anyone who follows me, will never walk in darkness, he will have the light of life."

In John 8:14-18 Jesus states, "Even if I testify on my own behalf, my testimony is valid, for I know where I came from and where I am going. But you have no idea where I come from or where I am going. You judge by human standards; I pass judgment on no one. But if I do judge, my decisions are right, because I am not alone. I stand with the Father, who sent me. In your own Law it is written that the testimony of two men is valid. 'Ego Eimi,' I am one who testifies for myself; my other witness is the Father, who sent me." I would say he is in pretty good company.

Jesus can witness without recourse to anyone else, except his Father. When we see the statement here, it's not as cool and as fun as the first couple of Scriptures, but boy, is it packed with depth and power. And it is because of who He is hanging out with. Because the Father did not leave Him. Later, we will see a place where Jesus is alone.

And what does He say? "Eli, Eli, lama Sabachthani?" "My God, My God, why have you forsaken me?" How can God separate Himself from God? He can't. But in that moment there were two people who prayed, "Father, let this cup pass from me. Nevertheless, not my will be done, but your will be done."

The first part of that prayer was the Son of Man. Part two of that prayer was the Son of God. The Son of Man hung dreadfully on that cross, and cried out, and the Father in heaven could not look, because Jesus in that moment bore my sin and your sin. And He cried out, "Eli, Eli, lama Sabachthani?" "Why, have you forsaken me?"

In that moment, He was alone and naked before all the world. And He cried out. That's what's going on here. He is his own self-sufficient witness. The Son of God never separated from God, the Father. But the Son of Man felt deserted and alone on that cross. The Son of Man and Son of God reunite in the tomb, in three days. Because God brought the Son of Man back to life, the Son of God never left, never died.

*Father in Jesus' name, we thank You Lord for Your hand upon us. I pray God that You would speak in ways that we cannot possibly fathom, to draw us close to You in all that we do. Your word, I pray, would penetrate our hearts, to their deepest recesses, and that you would speak to us. Let our savior be our light, every step that we take, every day, everywhere we go, we ask this and we give you praise and glory, in Jesus' name. Amen.*

# Chapter 6

# I Am (Part 2)

*Father in Jesus' name, we thank You, Lord, for Your direction, Your wisdom, for Your guidance, and Your presence this evening. I pray that Your Holy Spirit will guide our conversation, guide our hearts and our understanding, and we give You praise and glory for all that You do in Jesus' name, amen.*

I shared my testimony one time with a lady whose specialty is whether God speaks to people today. She had written an article by that title in their journal, and she asked me to sign up for a session over lunch time. This was in a doctoral program, which I ultimately could not complete. I signed up for the lunchtime session. I was like the resident Pentecostal/Charismatic person.

In a half an hour's time, I shared my story. When I finished, she said, "Wow! I knew God spoke to people like that, but I've never heard of anything like that since the thirteenth century."

She was talking about St. Teresa of Avila, the so-called dancing nun in Spain. There are instances of the outpouring of the Holy Spirit all the way through the history of the church. It didn't go away, and it didn't start at the dawn of the 20th century. Anyway, I shared my story with her and she was blown away by it. You never know where you're going to find those moments of powerful fellowship in the Lord, and it can be anywhere. And it ended with some serious fellowship with a serious Christian. And that's out of the blue. How do you know these things will happen? I did not expect that, and it surprised to find that was an exceptional moment. Jesus was a master at creating amazing moments just by being who He was.

To say this phrase, "I Am," at all is huge. Every time He used the phrase, it is about some unique aspect of who He is. We touched on the first three in the previous chapter. Let's continue from there.

These chapters come straight from the Scripture. On one side of me I have The New International Version and on the other side I have the Greek New Testament. I've taught this stuff before and it is real meat and potatoes. I hope you're able to receive a lot from that. We are in verse 23 of the eighth chapter of John. In the previous chapter we talked about testifying on His own behalf and His testimony is valid. In verse 19 the people asked, "Where is your father?" And He said, "you don't know Me or my Father." In verse 21 He said, "I'm going away, and you will look for me and you will die in your sin. Where I go you cannot come." This made the Jews ask, "Will he kill himself? Is that why he says, where I go, you cannot come?" But he continued, "You are from below. "Ego Eimi," I am from above." He uses that phrase for the fourth time. "I am from above." Then He uses it again. "You are of this world. Ego Eimi, I am not of this world. "I told you, that you would die in your sins if you do not believe that I am the one I claim to be. You will indeed die in your sins." He uses that phrase and He says it in a way that pairs Him with the Father. It makes Jesus part of the Godhead, all God and all man.

The Jews already had an awareness of the conversations in the Old Testament. They knew about, "Let us make man in our image" and "man and woman made He them." They also knew about, "Let us get them out of the garden before they could become like us and eat the fruit of the tree of life and live forever," because had they done that then they could not be cleansed from their sin because somebody had to die in their place. And if they can no longer die, then nobody can sacrifice for them and die in their place. Then we come forward to the conversation about

Jesus coming up out of the water and something appearing like a dove settled upon Him and a voice spoke from heaven and said, "This is my son in whom I'm well pleased."

Nowhere does it say Trinity. Everywhere Jesus uses this phrase, He self-identifies with the phrase used to identify the God of the burning bush of the Old Testament who led them out of Egypt. And He repeats Himself. The word, "ego," is "I" and then "eimi" is "I am." He is saying, "I, I am." He makes self-reference in a pronoun and then a verb that states self-existence. Do you get that? Does that make sense? That makes Him, just by saying that, to be self-identifying as God and that flipped the Pharisees out. They're thinking, "Blasphemy. How dare he say that?" As we go through this, then Jesus said to them, "Ego eimi going away. You will look for me and you will die in your sins. Where I go, you cannot come." Will He kill Himself?

"You are from below, but I am from above," is a pretty explicit reference. Jesus is not trying to be subtle about this." You are of this world. I am not of this world." Then He says, "I am from above," the positive, and "I am not of this world. I did not originate here," the negative. Now, a brief history. Do you remember when the angel showed up and said, "Blessed are you, Mary, because you've found favor with God"? She said, "I wonder what that means." Immediately, she got worried about it. Then he said, "Don't be afraid." But then after he explains to her what's going to happen, she says, "How will this be since I am a virgin?" And the angel explained, "The Holy Spirit will settle upon you," or "He will rest over you," however you want to look at it. It's like the Hebrew wording used in Genesis 1:2 when it says the Spirit of God hovered over the deep. The same Hebrew word also suggests a bird settling over her eggs in the nest.

It's an intimate connection. She will conceive from the Holy Spirit, not from Joseph or another human being. And the result of that is it sidesteps what we call the Adamic bloodline. The seed from the Holy Spirit is not from Adam. All other human beings have the seed that originated in the first place with Adam. Jesus is the sole exception. He is unique. There are a lot of speculators about whether or not Jesus is divine, or whether He was born from a virgin, who never had a sexual union with a human male. There are a lot of ideas about that. And some people try and say, "They might have gotten it from some cult virgin story." But there isn't one. It sprang up out of nothing. Nobody ever thought of that before because God never did it before.

It's important to know that, because you will have people try and suggest that something else happened in order to explain it away. There are many people who want to explain away the things of God, especially when it comes to origin issues. Where did Jesus come from? Was He God and man at the same time? We need to understand the power of what He is saying here. In that day and time, this is the same as saying, "I am God." However, He didn't come out and say it. He said, "I am from above. You don't know my father. I know him. I come from above. You're not from above. You're from down here. I am not from down here." He explains where He is from and then where He is not from. And in both cases, he uses "Ego eimi" to preface the statement.

"If you do not believe that I am the one I claim to be you will die in your sins." He had already answered this question. But it's interesting that they ask it anyway. "Who are you?" "Just what I have been claiming all along," Jesus replied. "I have much to say in judgment of you, but he who sent me is reliable and what I have heard from him, I tell the world." That's more or less the end of this episode. Then, His hearers could have said, "Jesus Said What?" because that's how they took it. "He blasphemed! Can you believe it?" They would not dare repeat "Ego Eimi," themselves, but it shook them up. His words created a huge stir and the episode is fascinating for that reason because some people say, "Jesus never said, 'I am God.'" This is about as close as He comes to saying, "I am God."

It's clear in the context and the choice of words, "Ego Eimi," being identical to the words used to translate from Hebrew into Greek for what God at the burning bush told Moses to say when he returned to Egypt. There is no accident to this. When Jesus said these things, He said them in a way that were not to be misconstrued or understood in any other way than what we see Him saying here.

The NIV version of the Bible highlights the title, "The Claims of Jesus About Himself." He talked to them about some things here. "Who would prove me guilty of sin? If I'm telling the truth, why don't you believe me?" In verse 48, the Jews answered Him, "Aren't we right in saying that you're a Samaritan and demon possessed?" Does that sound familiar in the political parlance of today? What is the human tendency to do to their opponents? It's to denigrate them, to accuse them of outlandish things. Humans do this all the time. And it doesn't matter what culture you find yourself in, what language you speak, it doesn't matter. This is what people do.

When people run out of actual things to talk about, principles or whatever, they resort to name calling and as an oversimplification, that's what this amounts to. So they say, "Aren't we right saying you're a Samaritan and are demon possessed?" Now what's wrong with the first one, calling Him a Samaritan.

They hated the Samaritans. Why? The Jews felt they were the chosen people, and the Samaritans were below them. Why did the Jews feel they were below them? There was some prejudice there, but why? Where did it come from? Where did it originate?

When they came out of Egypt, what did God tell them to do? What was the job description He gave the Jews through Moses? He told them to conquer all these peoples because they were all practicing pagan religions. They were sacrificing their babies on the altars to their gods, and they were doing all kinds of weird and bizarre things. He said, "Do not intermarry with them or take on their ways. Do not commit adultery with them, do not commit spiritual adultery." He called them out for combining other religious practices with their Jewish practices, which is referred to a syncretism. He referred to that as adultery as well as sexual union between someone other than your spouse. Jesus was vehement about that and said, "You go in here, do not intermarry with these people, do not adopt their religious practices, do not adopt their false Gods. I tell you, you need to conquer them because they have done things that are absolutely horrible and wicked in My sight." They had a job to do, to clear out the Promised Land, and they started out pretty well. The Battle of Jericho was the first battle fought by the Israelites in the course of the conquest of Canaan. But at some point, they ran out of steam. They avoided some people; they didn't confront them. But as they worked their way through, they sloughed it off and settled down with them and intermarried. Some of those were the Samaritans because they had retained a framework they saw as more or less Jewish in its origins, but they added a lot of other practices that were not Jewish and not ordained of God in their current practice.

So, the observant Jews would have nothing to do with them. They despised them because they intermarried, took false gods into their homes and into their hearts, and they adopted some of the religious practices God spoke against. That's the root of the difficulty with the Samaritans. That's why at another time, when Jesus sat down by the well, it was amazing, first of all, that he would sit there knowing it was in Samaria. Secondly, that He would speak to a woman at all. And third, that it was a Samaritan woman with whom He engaged in a meaningful conversation of consequence. He asked, "Where is your husband? You've had four or five already, but he is not even your husband." She said, "I see, you're a prophet." Little did she know.

And He said, "I can give you water that lasts for eternal life." She said, "I want some of that water." She ran into town and said, "You have to come hear this guy." And we know the rest of the story. But they generally avoided interactions with Samaritans at all costs, and to call someone a Samaritan was a deep insult. The reasons for that were for the most part in the perception of many buried in history. They didn't know why because that's how that stuff goes. It becomes ingrained and nobody can remember where it started and that's as true today as much as it ever was. Again, it's another part of the human condition about how we evaluate people. This was no small insult to accuse Him of being a Samaritan.

He said, "I'm not possessed by a demon." Notice that He deals with the two in reverse order. He didn't deal with the racial insult to start with. He said, "I'm not possessed by a demon, but I honor my father and you dishonor me." Here is that vertical reference again. See what He is doing? His father is not Joseph. He is not talking about him. He is not telling them about the Holy Spirit overshadowing His mother. But He speaks clearly. "I honor my Father and you dishonor me. I'm not seeking glory for Myself. But there is One who seeks it, and He is the judge as the Father. I tell you the truth. If anyone keeps My word, he will never see death."

At this, the Jews exclaimed, "Now we know, you are demon possessed. Abraham died and so did the prophets, yet you say that if anyone keeps your word, he will never taste death. Are you greater than our father Abraham? He died and so did the prophets. Who do you think you are?" That's a fair question. I mean, they're being asked to accept a lot at face value with no other evidence except He is telling them this. Who do you think you are? Jesus replied, "If I glorify myself, my glory means nothing. My father, whom you claim as your God, is the one who glorifies me." Do you see the reference He makes there? The connection. "My father who you claim as your God." Did you catch that? He didn't say, my father who is your God, but who you claim as your God.

Now, let's parse that and see what that means. "Who you claim as your God." What did He just say? Saying it doesn't make it right. Jesus said it in a way that didn't outright question it, but He puts them in a position of having to defend their claim that His father is their God. Jesus does one more thing when He says, "My father whom you claim… ." He identifies with who they think is their God, and He did not affirm that His Father is their God. They may claim it. Again, Jesus makes good use of language. Remember, the whole thing is about language and use of words. We must understand what is being said to get it inside us, to own it.

There was a young man named Cameron who I used to teach at Wednesday night class when church was over. It was a second Wednesday night class. We had some guys there who were interested in going deeper with the Lord and ministry. Brother Bob Buchanan was also there, and he loved it. He studied philosophy. And he said, "Man, I enjoy your teaching." I said, "I sure enjoy your contributions, too." We had a beautiful relationship in that regard. He was in his eighties. Cameron got his Master of Divinity degree from Liberty University and became a chaplain candidate. He went over to Japan with his wife. He used to teach young adults at our church. In Japan, he planted a church. When his Air Force wife transferred over to Landstuhl, Germany, he did ministry over there. When she transferred to the East Coast somewhere, Cameron became a Civil Air Patrol Chaplain. Those Wednesday night sessions met a need.

I was told later by Brother B that I was using the Socratic method. Somebody in the group would throw something out like, "Didn't the Bible say, such-and-such?"

I would say, "Does it? Show me."

And then they would dig it up with what they thought the Bible said and it turned out it didn't say what they thought it did. We would discover another part, or what we assumed to be another part, somewhere else. Then we would talk about the connections between the two. We discovered together that language is important. We need to understand that the thoughts expressed have meaning.

I told one young man, who was part of that group, "Words have power."

He said "No, they don't, they're only words."

I said, "Here is what I want you to do. I want you to look up Matthew 12:36-37. Then I want you to come back next week and tell me that words don't have power and prove it."

Jesus said, "But I tell you that men will have to give account on the day of judgment for every careless word they have spoken. For by your words you will be acquitted, and by your words you will be condemned."

That's powerful when you stop and think about it because every careless word that proceeds from your mouth is an important concept and it's worth dwelling on for a second here because of what we're talking about. What are careless words? How often have you carelessly said something and threw it out in the heat of the moment? You instantly wished you hadn't said it or maybe you double down or you're glad you said it. But we all have said things we regretted as soon as we said them.

Carl Sandburg, the American poet, said, "Look out how you use proud words. When you let proud words go, it is not easy to call them back. They wear long boots, hard boots; they walk off proud; they can't hear you calling. Look out how you use proud words."

You can't unsay stuff because it's in everybody's ears and their head. You can't un-ring the bell. It's important to realize that. The whole concept is that you're either acquitted or condemned, not by your planned out words, your thoughts through words, your carefully framed words, but your careless words. Why? Because the careless words are closer to your heart in what you mean. In the last part of Luke 6:45 Jesus said, "For out of the overflow of his heart his mouth speaks." In Luke 6:43 Jesus also talked about fruit in the same way, "No good tree bears bad fruit, nor does a bad tree bear good fruit."

It's a powerful concept found in Scripture and discussed by Jesus at various points. He talks about, "I'm the true vine, you're the branches." This is important when you think about it. And words are part of that. Words are part of the way with which we can communicate with each other, and we have to be careful how we communicate. I would say something to one of my children, most likely my son.

I would ask, "Why did you do it?"

He would answer, "I was just curious what would happen if I did that."

He once took a paperclip, unbent it, and stuck it into an electrical outlet because he wanted to see what would happen. It threw a breaker off, and hence he said, "I only wanted to see what happened."

I said, "That was pretty stupid."

He said, "I'm not stupid."

My reply? "I didn't say you are stupid, but what you did was stupid. I didn't mean you're stupid but everybody, no matter how smart or dumb you are, we're all capable of doing stupid stuff."

I always tried to be careful to clarify my words if there was ever any question.

I flat out told him, "That's one of the dumbest things you've ever done."

And he was like, "I'm not dumb."

Words have power. And of course Jesus knew that better than anyone. Why? Because he never wrote anything on Earth that we know of. We certainly don't have a copy. But He is the author and finisher of our faith. He is the author of the word of God right from the beginning because He took part in every action and everything that takes place throughout the word of God from the beginning. Do you get that? In John 1:1 the Bible says, "In the beginning was the word, and the word was with God and the word was God." Words, language, things being expressed are important.

We find the fifth I Am statement of Jesus in John 8:54-58 and it represents the first time it caused a physical threat on His life.

> Jesus said, "If I glorify myself, my glory means nothing. My Father, whom you claim as your God, is the one who glorifies me. Though you do not know him, I know him. If I said I did not, I would be a liar like you, but

I do know him and keep his word. Your father Abraham rejoiced at the thought of seeing my day; he saw it and was glad." "You are not yet fifty years old," the Jews said to him, "and you have seen Abraham!" "I tell you the truth," Jesus answered, "before Abraham was born, I am!"

What did He do? Right there in the middle of one word, He goes this way and then, Bam! He takes a hard turn. "Before Abraham was born, ego eimi, I am." Now, I'm going to use a phrase that I claimed. I've heard nobody else use it, therefore I claim it as mine. Maybe somebody else said it to me and I said it out of the blue. But the phrase is a simple, three words: "Eternity is now." Or you can shorten it and say, "Eternity is." But eternity is now. Eternity does not know past, present, and future in the same sense we do. Do you understand that? Let me explain it. I don't know that you do, but I want you to get it. This is important. God is eternal. The first words of Jesus in the Revelation confirm this as found in 1:8, "I am the Alpha and the Omega," says the Lord God, "who is, and who was, and who is to come, the Almighty."

There is no beginning and there is no end because He is the beginning. Everything emanates from God. He preexists all of it and has no beginning.

Eternity has no beginning and no end. You got that part? How then can we accede to eternal life? God is eternal. We at some point start toward eternal life. That's when we enter into relationship with the King of kings and Lord of lords. Make sense? When I say, "eternity is now," it is not subject to the vagaries of time. It is not subject to space. It is not subject to any of these existential limitations where we find ourselves ensconced. You and I live in time. We are creatures of time. And we will be until we become like Him. In First Corinthians 13:12 Paul says, "Now we see but a poor reflection as in a mirror; then we shall see face to face." In First John Chapter 3:2b-3 it says, "But we know that when he appears, we shall be like him, for we shall see him as he is. Everyone who has this hope in him purifies himself, just as he is pure." The

Bible makes reference to this in Second Corinthians 3:18, "And we, who with unveiled faces all reflect the Lord's glory, are being transformed into his likeness with ever-increasing glory, which comes from the Lord, who is the Spirit." We're growing toward that place, but we're not there in this world, in this life. We are already recipients of His matchless grace, but not yet grown into His inimitable glory. Already not yet.

Take hold of your Bible. Close it, but keep your finger there. Now that Bible is your life. Everybody has a life. God lives outside of your life. You started your life at page one and progressed one page at a time through that book, through life to where you are now. Jesus is writing, and He wrote the book called The Bible. But here is something you can't do. You must go to the next page and then to the next page and then to the next page. God can come and stick His finger anywhere and open it up to whatever page He wants to, whenever He deems it necessary, because He is outside of time. He is eternal. He surrounds time. Does this make sense? This is not simple stuff, is it? They are things we need to understand.

C.S. Lewis wrote a book called *Miracles*. And the way he explains the miraculous is that God momentarily intercedes with something completely outside of anything in nature or natural possibility, a miracle. But then, everything goes back to normal and continues on in this world under its natural and physical laws. God can heal a person in an instant. That's a miracle. And yet God at that point, sticks His finger right at that page and heals you, but then you continue living.

There was an older lady in the congregation in North Dakota where I pastored. Her son was a chief of police in the state police force in South Dakota. When he was a kid, he was being cute in the kitchen and he stood on one of the round kitchen tables that was on a pedestal. He went over the edge, banged up his knee, and couldn't move. He couldn't put any weight on his knee. His mother and father came together and laid hands on him, which is what they always did. They prayed, and he hopped up and ran outside. There was no more pain. Now, at 45-years-old, his superiors recommended him for promotion to a senior position in the state police in South Dakota. They had to do an entire physical screen. They took a picture of his knee and found that there was a fine fracture line on that knee. Although it healed, the fracture was discernible.

They asked, "When did you break your knee?"

He said, "I never broke my knee. What are you talking about?"

"It's right there on the X-ray. See that line?" "

Yeah, but I don't remember that."

He went home, and he talked to his mom about it and she said, "Well, you fell off the kitchen table and we prayed for you because you couldn't move your knee or put weight on it. After we prayed, you ran off to go play. You never had another problem with it."

I mean, how often does it happen when you do something because God says trust Him for it and it happens? How powerful is that? Now I tire of it when folks go through all these machinations with whatever ails them or vexes them. And you hear these testimonies where they say, "I had this illness, and I went to the doctor and the doctor didn't know what to do. Then I went to a specialist and the specialist couldn't figure it out and said it could be several things and maybe I need some experimental medicine. I went to somebody else, and they said blah, blah, blah. Out of desperation, I went forward at this crusade (in service or in a church, whatever). Somebody prayed, and I was healed. Halleluiah, praise God, thank You, Jesus!" My question is, "Why didn't you pray and believe to begin with?" I know everybody doesn't pray to begin with. Many people do. But the point is, if we always trust God first and then let man do what man will do, God will still get the glory.

I remember when we prayed for a little boy about five or six years old. He was in Minnesota, and we were in North Dakota. A lady in our congregation said, "We have some dear friends whose six-year-old boy has a brain aneurysm, and the doctors scheduled a delicate surgery for Monday."

We prayed. I said, "Father, I pray in Jesus' name that You would dissolve away any of the bad stuff that's there. Father, I pray that You bring healing for the underlying cause, as well as the symptoms, and that you would dissolve anything harmful and that You would give the doctors guidance and wisdom. help them know what to do. It is my prayer that You would astonish family, friends, doctors, nurses, and medical staff. I pray that we lift Your name up and glorify You whatever happens. We thank You and praise You in Jesus' name." That was essentially the prayer I prayed.

When Monday arrived, they delayed the little boy's surgery because another little boy had a sudden urgent emergency, also a brain aneurysm. They took care of that boy. He was on the table for eight or ten hours. When they got to the little boy we had prayed for, they shaved the spot, cut the hole in his skull, and they found a little round disc sitting right there on top of his brain. They picked it up and there was nothing else. The brain aneurysm had disappeared.

Can you imagine that? Can you imagine how big a God we serve that is this kind? He knows His Father. That's why this stuff with words matters. And when before Abraham was born, past tense, "I am," eternal. Get it? Eternity is now. God stuck His finger in that little boy's book and healed him, and then he went on with his life.

But sometimes He doesn't. You can pray whatever you want, and that's the point. We need to trust and believe God knows what's going on. It's way too easy. God knows, you know, and that's not comfort. But we still need to make it a practice of trusting Him first. That doesn't mean it's always going to work out the way we want it to. The way we want it isn't always the answer God gives or what we need to receive, whatever it may be.

I mean, I sure wish our week in our motor home would have been a lot easier. But it was hard. That was our first time. I had told people about our maiden voyage, but we had one problem after another. We didn't even get out of town before the engine overheated. We were traveling to my fiftieth high school reunion, where I was to play as the featured soloist for a concert with the high school band. I thought, *I'm going to miss this concert.*

We called the Good Sam Club, and they sent a guy out and he came and I talked to the guy at Spartan, who makes the chassis and I thought it was a coolant issue.

He said, "No, I don't think it's a coolant issue."

I said "We're turning around to get in this empty lot so we'll be able to get out of it when the time comes and the steering w as sludgy."

The Spartan guy said, "Ah, hah, see, it's hydraulic. That can cause it to overheat. That must be it."

It turns out when the guy from the Good Sam Club got there, it was neither the coolant nor hydraulics. Apparently, the RV had gone over a rock or something and bashed in the cowling over the fan. The radiator is on the side and it pressed the fan cowling up against the fan blades. It couldn't turn to cool the engine.

He got in there, cut out a piece that was in the way, to keep it from being impinged, and we never had another problem with it overheating. But that doesn't mean we didn't have another problem for the entire trip. We couldn't get our bedroom slide to go out. We had to crawl over the bed to get in. And another guy who had been RVing longer term, came over and we dismantled the part that caused the problem.

The last two nights we were there, we could sleep in a regular bed and walk around instead of having to crawl over to get into the closet on our hands and knees. It was difficult. Our bus needs 50 amp service, but the site only had 30 amp service.

I put it on an adapter, but it kept throwing out the circuit breaker and it wouldn't run the AC. We sweltered. We had to open windows to get cross circulation and finally cool off before we go to sleep. You know that saying, "It's just one thing after another." But we learned to figure some things out. I said, "God make this a perfect trip," but it wasn't. You never know what He is going to do. That's a low-key milder version of what can happen. But the point is it's not what He does, it's Who He is. And that's the part that we're focused on here. "Before Abraham was, I am." That made a statement because He went from past tense to eternity. "Eternity is now." It never has a past, present, or future.

For the sixth I Am statement, let's move over to the 10th chapter of John and see what we can find there. We want to get to the shepherd and his flock. John 10:1 begins, "I tell you the truth." Do you know the story well? This is the story of the good shepherd. "I will tell you the truth" right at verse one. "The man who does not enter the sheep pen by the gate but climbs in by some other way is a thief and a robber."

Otherwise, why wouldn't he just go in the main entrance? "The man who enters by the gate is the shepherd of his sheep. The watchman opens the gate for him and the sheep listen to his voice. He calls his own sheep by name and leads them out."

"When he has brought out all of his own, he goes on ahead of them and his sheep follow him because they know his voice. But they will never follow a stranger. In fact, they will run away from him because they do not recognize a stranger's voice." I was stationed in Frankfurt, Germany, with the Third Armored Division Band. They had an Association of the United States Army conference and they scheduled the band to go down to Garmisch—Partenkirchen, in southern Germany to play for the event. Located in a ski town of Bavaria, the mountain area is beautiful. We did a concert and a couple of ceremonies.

We had an afternoon free. I and three other guys took a stroll up the side of the mountain. We went into town, got some cheese and some other items from a local store and then we took off. As we walked up the mountain, we saw a fenced in area with real thin wire, and it turned out to be electrical. You didn't touch that twice. The sheep there most likely already knew that. Anyway, I tried to call them over to grab a handful of grass or something and they came over at first, nibbled a little. After a while they lost interest and walked away.

We went on uphill, had a good time, and found a nice mountain stream. It was real cold water. Ice and snow still melted off in the spring weather. We climbed further up the mountain, a nice scenic hike, then climbed back down by the same way. We came to that same meadow with the sheep and we tried to call them again but they ignored us. They didn't look at us at all. That's right here in our passage. They will not follow a stranger. In fact, they will run away from a stranger because they did not know his voice. That sets the stage for what He is about to tell them.

Therefore, Jesus said, "I tell you the truth. Ego eimi, I am the gate for the sheep. All who ever came before me were thieves and robbers. But the sheep did not listen to them. Ego eimi, I am the gate. Whoever enters through me will be saved. He will come in and go out and find pasture. The thief comes only to steal and kill and destroy. I have come that they may have life and have it to the full." That's the first section. Let's see if we can wrap our minds around this. In the wilderness, often the shepherd would build a little pen of stakes and branches or bushes as available. Then he would lay down across the opening so that if anything or anyone came in, he would awaken and be able to protect the sheep.

He was the sheep gate. He slept with the sheep inside the pen that he had built and he became the gate, the entranceway, through whom they must enter. Anybody who comes in any other way trying to sneak in would have to go through a wall of stakes and branches. Obviously, he could not do it without making a lot of noise and racket. Not to mention that those sheep will make a lot of noise, too, because they know it's not him. He is the path by which non-interlopers must come. Anybody who comes in any other way is a thief and a robber. That seems pretty obvious.

That's why He claims "ego eimi, the sheep gate." "I am the gate by which they come and go." That's pretty straightforward. Then he uses the same phrase he used before, "Ego eimi, I am the good shepherd." "The good shepherd lays down his life for the sheep. The hired hand is not the shepherd who owns the sheep. When he sees the wolf coming, he abandons the sheep and runs away. Then the wolf attacks the flock and scatters it. The man runs away because he is a hired hand and cares nothing for the sheep."

How often do we see examples of that in life? "Not me. I don't own the store, why should I bother? Hey, you can have all this money if you want." Every once in a while you see somebody in a stick up. There was a guy in the news who worked in a little convenience store. A holdup man stuck a gun in his face and he disarmed the guy. He grabbed the gun and pointed it away and wrestled him around and he wouldn't let him have the money. He fought for the store. But you know that's rare. Well, he didn't own it, but most people won't do that.

Maybe they won't fight because maybe the owners have insurance and they will get the money back. That's how most of us deal with it. "Our insurance will pay for it. Don't worry about this. Just give me the money." The point is if you own it, you're probably going to defend it with more vigor. Anyway, the wolf attacks and the flock and scatters. The man runs away because he is a hired hand and cares nothing for the sheep. And there it is right there, "cares nothing for the sheep." We're not talking about cash and a cash register here. We're talking about relationships.

In the first portion, the sheep know their master's voice and they follow him and they don't know a stranger's voice and will not follow the stranger. Now we're talking about a relationship. The man runs away because he is a hired hand and cares nothing for the sheep. In Luke 15 Jesus tells the story of the 99 and the one and He hits on this exact point. He leaves the 99 and goes to find the one lost sheep. He uses his crook because he can reach down if one has fallen down a cliff or something like that. He can hook him under the forelegs and bring him back up. That's a rescue tool, not because he needs help walking around, but it's a tool in his trade.

In North Dakota, they began giving out crooks after they ordained me, therefore I didn't get one. I got an ordination Bible, but I didn't get the crook. But the District Superintendent began giving a crook to all the new pastors he put in place. And the whole point is, as a pastor you have to defend the sheep and you will use the crook to rescue the sheep from time to time. The issue here becomes about relationship. "Cares nothing for the sheep." Now the sheep have an interesting interrelationship with each other as well. But they have to follow something or someone. Generally, that's why you have sheepdogs to keep them in line and get them to go places.

In the movie "Charlotte's Web," it is interesting to watch the pig do what a sheepdog would normally do. But sheep aren't leaders, they are followers. Sheepdogs bark and nip at their heels, do whatever it takes to get them where they're supposed to go or keep them where they should stay. In Charlotte's Web, it turned out the pig did a better job than any dog because the pig could talk to the sheep. But sheep need to be led somewhere. We as human beings need to be led somewhere.

And guess who is going to do that? In the next paragraph, Jesus says, "Ego eimi, I am the good shepherd. I know my sheep and my sheep know me. Just as the father knows me and I know the father and I laid down my life for the sheep. I have other sheep that are not of this sheep pen." By the way, I got hit with that in verse 16. I was talking with a guy in Germany who was a member of the Latter-Day Saints (LDS). He called this verse to my attention, and he said, "So then Jesus revealed himself to the Latter-Day Saints over in North America, couldn't that be what He was talking about?"

I said, "I don't think so. He will not give you a different and new revelation that undoes everything He did and said before. It's not consistent. And if God is anything, He is consistent with

Himself. God is the same yesterday, today, and forever. He is the one who is from the beginning. He is Alpha and Omega, the beginning and the end, all those characteristics. It does not follow in light of this that we should accept this verse as proof for this so-called appearance or alleged appearance in North America to Joseph Smith." My answer to him was "no," for those reasons. But the point is in verse 16. "I have other sheep that are not of this sheep pen. I must bring them also."

There is a concept that I have of the body of Christ which holds that it is trans-historical, trans-generational, as well as trans-geographic. It's across many things. And God's relationship with His sheep crosses time, centuries, and they cross geographical barriers. I believe anybody who cries out to God and asks Him, "Lord, reveal yourself to me," can expect that He can and He will do it in the deepest corners of the world, in jungles and swamps, high deserts and mountains, and anywhere you find yourself in a city, a country setting, different social areas, in this vast world of His creation.

It doesn't matter who you are or where you are from. Look at Corrie ten Boom. Do you know her story? Corrie ten Boom wasn't the spiritual one. Her older sister, Elizabeth, was. Their father, Casper, was a watchmaker in Holland. When the Germans took over and they started coming down on the Jews, they helped the Jews hide and then helped them make their way out of Holland away from Nazi occupation. They got found out and the entire family from their elderly father all the way down were put in concentration camps. Corrie was kind of cantankerous about it. During the last days of their imprisonment, Elizabeth said God told her that the both of them would be free of the concentration camp before the year 1945. On December 16, 1944, Elizabeth died. On December 30, 1944, because of a mysterious clerical error, out of the blue, they released Corrie from the prison camp. Nobody to this day knows why. She walked out the front gate of this prison. From that moment forward, she told the story of Jesus. She wrote books and spoke wherever she could and remembered what her sister told her.

She took to heart what her sister did as much as what her sister said because she would give her last grains of rice to anyone who needed it more than she did. Corrie learned from her sister that it's all about relationships. God reached out to her, moved things around so that she would get released, and then gave her an amazing story. My wife has all of her books, one of which is *Not Good if Detached*. In it she tells the story of a ticket to get on the subway, one half of which is marked not good if detached. If you're detached from Jesus, you're "not good if detached." When it comes to relationship, Jesus says, "I have other sheep that are not of this pen. I must bring them also." He reaches across time and He reaches across geography. He reaches across ethnic and cultural barriers.

God can reach across every kind of barrier you can imagine. He can reach across that barrier and it doesn't matter about distance or anything else if you cry out to God. He is saying, "There are many others and they, too, will listen to my voice. There shall be one flock and one shepherd. The reason My Father loves Me is that I lay down My life only to take it up again. No one takes it from Me, but I lay it down of my own accord." He says, "It was my idea. I didn't have it taken from me, nobody fooled me into giving it up, it was something I decided to do." Jesus came down knowing full well what awaited Him.

Now, I don't know when in His earthly life as a young boy He became aware of who He was. We find him in the temple as he talked with the elders and answered questions that surprised and astonished everybody. Over time, he grew up into the man He became. We don't understand that is the coming of age of the Son of Man and coming of awareness of the Son of God. Does that make sense? Both became part of who He was in full measure. Here He says, "I lay down my life, no one takes it from me." Nobody took Jesus' life from Him. "I lay it down of my own accord. I have authority to lay it down and authority to take it up again. This command I received from my Father." This comes out of the saying, "I am the good shepherd."

And it's established on relationship and He has His relationship in more than one place. "I have other sheep not of this pen. I must bring them as well. They will listen to my voice as well and there shall be in the end one flock and one shepherd where we get to know each other." Is that cool or what? There is only one flock and one shepherd and one book.

The word "authority" is in verse 18. Exousia is the word. There are different words for power. There is the one word, Dunamis, where we get the word dynamite. Alfred Nobel is the inventor of dynamite. It got used and abused as a weapon of war. He tried to find a more stable way to transport nitroglycerin. He soaked it into silica, a malleable paste, and developed dynamite. The Greek word implies explosive power, and that's why he thought it was appropriate to call it that. There is also Kratos. Do you remember Arnold Schwarzenegger in his prime? Anybody want to arm wrestle him when he was in his prime? When you looked at him, you could see power waiting to move into action. That's Kratos. You get it? You can see the power.

Exousia is another word for power and its power that is based on authority. When a person walks up and he has a uniform on and a badge, you know he has authority. Does that make sense? It's apparent. If a person walks up without a badge and starts telling you what to do, you will not likely pay attention as much. But the guy with a badge, and the car, with lights and writing on it, he whips out a piece of paper and he writes a ticket because he has authority, Exousia.

Jesus says, "I have authority to lay it down and take it up again." He is saying, "I can die on the cross, but then I can rise again." Do you see what He is talking about? He points straight toward the empty tomb. Now the Father resurrected His son, but the point is, He received this command from His Father. The

Father authorized Him to do what He came to do. This is not the same as the resurrection of Lazarus. In both cases, Jesus and Lazarus, the authority, exousia, was with Jesus to bring about resurrection.

Now in the Garden of Gethsemane, two men prayed. Do you know who they were? Jesus and Jesus. The Son of Man said, "Father, let this cup pass from me." But the Son of God said, "Nevertheless, not my will, but thy will be done." This is the balance and the struggle. This is the thing that Jesus came to be and to do. And He tells us, "No one takes my life from me, I lay it down of my own accord. I have Exousia, the power of authority. Authority comes from something, someone, somewhere. And in this case, it comes from the Father. "I have authority to lay it down and authority to take it up again." That's not a small thing to lay down life and take it up again. "This command I received from my father." They went away wagging their heads and saying He was a demon possessed, raving man. Why listen to it? They didn't get it.

But some did. John was smart enough to write it down. Any questions? Let's pray. Father in Jesus' name, thank You Lord, for Your word, thank You for Your son, thank You for Your Holy Spirit, thank You for Your amazing love for us. First John 3:1, tells us, "Behold, what manner of love the Father hath bestowed upon us, that we should be called the sons of God: therefore the world knoweth us not, because it knew him not."

*Father, thank You for loving us and making us Your children. I pray that these things we spoke of, the words we continue to uncover in our journey of hearing what Jesus said, I pray they would speak to our lives afresh and anew, and the power of those words would come to life in the midst of our being, Father. I pray You would help our hearts and our minds to absorb as You give to us and nourish us by what You share with us. We thank you. We praise you in the marvelous name of Your Son, Jesus Christ, amen and amen. God bless you.*

# Chapter 7

# Final Statements

*Heavenly Father, we thank You for Your Son, whom You sent for our salvation. Guide our hearts as we conclude our study of His "I Am" statements in the book of John. Please touch our hearts and minds to truly grasp the significance of these moments in His earthly ministry and their impact on our earthly lives over 2,000 years later. We give You praise in advance for what we are about to read and study, in Jesus' name, Amen.*

In John chapter 10, Jesus was in Jerusalem when the Jews asked Him, "How long will you keep us in suspense? If you are the Christ, tell us plainly." He tried to tell them He had already told them but that they did not want to hear it. Then He said, "I and the Father are one" (John 10:30, NIV). In the next verse, the crowd picked up stones to stone Him. He asked them for which of the miracles he had done in their midst were they going to stone Him? Their reply was revealing, "We are not stoning you for any of these," replied the Jews, "but for blasphemy, because you, a mere man, claim to be God." They understood His statement, that He and the Father are one, to mean that He claimed to be God.

In the 11th chapter of John then, Jesus and His disciples received news from Mary and Martha in Bethany that Lazarus was sick and expected to die. In John 11:4 Jesus' response was,

"This sickness will not end in death. No, it is for God's glory that God's Son may be glorified through it."

This is a revealing statement on several levels. First of all, Jesus reveals that He already knew of Lazarus' illness, and not only was aware of it but aware of the course it would take. When He said, "it will not end in death," it may not have been clear to the disciples that Lazarus would indeed die. But Jesus is speaking in a prescient manner of the fact that Lazarus will die, but he would not stay dead.

Secondly, Jesus indicates that Lazarus' illness will be a vehicle that would reveal God's glory. He does not specify how, but it points to something that is not associated with someone's illness and death.

Thirdly, He reveals it is also for the glory of God's Son. Jesus offers no further clarification at this point. They stayed where they were for two more days, after which Jesus said, "Let us go back to Judea." When His disciples took exception to the idea of returning to Judea, He said, "Our friend Lazarus has fallen asleep; but I am going there to wake him up." The disciples thought He meant actual sleep, therefore Jesus explained, "Lazarus is dead, and for your sake I am glad I was not there, so that you may believe. But let us go to him."

The disciples took a somewhat fatalistic view of that decision. They remembered when the crowd recently tried to stone Him, they said, "Let us also go, that we may die with him."

When they arrived in Bethany, they learned that Lazarus had already been in the tomb for four days. Then Martha came out to meet Jesus, and she said, "Lord, if you had been here, my brother would not have died. But I know that even now God will give you whatever you ask." Jesus told her that her brother would rise again, but she took the long view and said, "I know he will rise again in the resurrection at the last day."

And here we find the next statement of Jesus in John 11:25-26. "Jesus said to her, '(Ego eimi), I Am the resurrection and the life. He who believes in me will live, even though he dies; and whoever lives and believes in me will never die. Do you believe this?'" Of course, Martha replied in the affirmative, and then went home and told Mary where Jesus was. Mary came out to meet Him and said the same thing Martha had said about her brother not dying had Jesus been there.

Jesus saw Mary and those who also mourned and wept, and He was "deeply moved in spirit and troubled." He asked where Lazarus had been laid. When they took Him to the tomb site, it says, "Jesus wept."

Having said that, it is worth unpacking what we have so far.

In verse 25 Jesus said, "(Ego eimi) I Am the resurrection and the life." This statement of eternal existence now turns around Martha's answer to His question. She said that she believed her brother would raise up "at the last day," referring to the eschatological "not yet" end of time on this earth. Jesus makes resurrection immediate in effect and fully realized in His existence. The Greek word for resurrection is anastasis. Stasis means static or inert, frozen in time. The preface, ana, negates that, meaning not static or inert, no longer frozen in time. To make sure He drives the point home, He adds, kai zoe, and life, so that not only is one no longer inert in death, but animated in life. Zoe is the word from which we get zoology, the study of animal, therefore animate, life.

The unfolding events leading up to this monumental statement and to the aftermath at the tomb are a remarkable view of Jesus' intense and boundless compassion, both in His earthly existence and in His eternal state of being. The temporal tragedy of death coupled with the glorious victory of eternal life that the grave cannot contain profoundly moves Him. Those who heard them immediately realized the power of the words when

Jesus says, "Lazarus, come out!" Many have opined that it was a good thing that Jesus had specified Lazarus or there would have followed a scene with dozens or hundreds of entombed bodies being reanimated and walking out of their tombs.

We find the next I Am statement in John 14:5-6. "Thomas said to Him, 'Lord, we don't know where you are going, so how can we know the way?' Jesus answered, '(Ego eimi) I am the way and the truth and the life. No one comes to the Father except through me.'" Once again, the eternal immediacy of that phrase, ego eimi, I Am, lends itself to another aspect of Jesus. The threefold self-reference He makes here begins with a word that means, way, road, or path. It is difficult to know whether Thomas thought there was a literal road to a person or place that directions could get him to. It does not seem likely that he thought that, however, because by then he knew a lot about who Jesus was and His origin. Most likely Thomas was wrestling with understanding that origin and how to get there. Jesus' answer, however, went beyond what Thomas expected. Jesus used the same word, odon (way, road, or path), that Thomas used, but amplified it with two other terms. However, by using ego eimi, I am, Jesus redefines that word by making Jesus the way, road, or path, which suggests further examination.

In Mark 8:34-35 we read, "Then He called the crowd to Him along with His disciples and said: 'If anyone would come after Me, he must deny himself and take up his cross and follow Me. For whoever wants to save his life will lose it, but whoever loses his life for Me and for the gospel will save it.'" Thomas was familiar with what Jesus had said here, but it may not have occurred to him that this was, at least in part, the answer to his question of Jesus. The way was not a what or a where, but a who. And of course, not just a who, but the ultimate Who. Thomas may not have realized that he asked for directions to the right hand of the Father.

The next sign-post, so to speak, is the truth. Once again, a distinction must is needed. We are not only talking about always telling the truth and being honest. By saying ego eimi, I Am the truth, Jesus becomes the truth against which we measured all else for truth. Truth becomes a Who. Truth binds the way, road, or path on all sides.

The third part of this ego eimi statement, I Am the life, ties the three together. These three elements provide an insight to Jesus' nature that is unique in Scripture. He says He is the way, road, or path that is defined and bounded by absolute truth of which He is the perfect expression, and the source of all life. The writer of Hebrews may give us some insight into the immensity of this simple, three-part statement.

> "In the past God spoke to our forefathers through the prophets at many times and in various ways, but in these last days he has spoken to us by his Son, whom he appointed heir of all things, and through whom he made the universe. The Son is the radiance of God's glory and the exact representation of his being, sustaining all things by his powerful word. After he had provided purification for sins, he sat down at the right hand of the Majesty in heaven. So he became as much superior to the angels as the name he has inherited is superior to theirs," (Hebrews 1:1–4, NIV).

This brings us to the second part of Jesus' message, "No one comes to the Father except through me." After articulating His being as the way, the truth, and the life, He now clarifies that this is absolutely unique. He is the only access to the Father. Any attempt to come to the Father by any other means will fail. God has provided only one, and that is through His monogeneis, only begotten, Son.

Another statement gives a better understanding of the working relationship between Jesus and His Father, and our relationship with Jesus. We find the first in John 15:1, "(Ego eimi), I am the true vine, and my Father is the gardener." This relationship between Son and Father is simple. Jesus is the true vine, and His Father cares for that vine just as a gardener would. It is possible that Jesus was walking through a vineyard with His disciples when He shared these two closely related "I Am" statements. Theirs was an agrarian culture and they would have been familiar with this illustration, or parable. The first public miracle performed by Jesus was when He turned water into wine at the wedding feast at Cana, recorded only in John's gospel. A gardener pays close attention to the weather, the seasons, how the plants he tends appears, and so on. Jesus' use of the phrase, "I am the true vine," indicates the uniqueness of His nature. There are many vines, but only one true vine. Not only that, but the Father tends only to the nurture and growth of the true vine.

The second relationship is in John 15:5, "(Ego eimi), I am the vine; you are the branches. If a man remains in Me and I in him, he will bear much fruit; apart from Me you can do nothing."

Jesus is the vine here, which means He is the primary connection we branches have to the nourishing soil upon which we depend for our function and existence. Then we are the sole connection to the nurturing from Jesus for the fruit we bear. The vine extracts nourishment from the soil through its root structures and passes it along to all the branches.

The clear emphasis here is not on Jesus doing His job, but on us fulfilling our responsibilities. Our goal is for us to bear much fruit. At first glance, our job as a branch seems pretty simple, but that can be deceptive. Our job is to remain in Jesus, the vine, and allow Him to remain in us. If we fulfill that, the expectation is that we will bear much fruit.

There appear to be two potential points of failure for us. One is failure to remain in Jesus, and the other is failure to allow Jesus to remain in us. Jesus did not say for us to remain in Him *or* allow Him to remain in us, but for us to remain in Him *and* allow Him to remain in us. He sums failure to do either one as, "apart from me you can do nothing." Either failure separates us from Him and causes an inability to produce fruit.

Here we define the word for fruit as fruit, crop, harvest, or produce of vegetation, and by extension, deed, activity, or produce of a person. In this context, the extension part of the definition applies.

To begin with, no pun intended, referring to the sixth day of creation in Genesis 1:28 we read, "God blessed them and said to them, 'Be fruitful and increase in number; fill the earth and subdue it.'" The initial blessing God pronounced on the first humans He created called for them to be fruitful, that is to reproduce, with the goal of filling and subduing the earth. This would seem to be a literal understanding of fruit as produce of a person from the above definition. This began the first covenant, also known to us as the Old Testament.

More suitable to the New Testament, or the New Covenant, would be this passage in 2 Corinthians 5:16-19:

> "So from now on we regard no one from a worldly point of view. Though we once regarded Christ in this way, we do so no longer. Therefore, if anyone is in Christ, he is a new creation; the old has gone, the new has come! All this is from God, who reconciled us to himself through Christ and gave us the ministry of reconciliation: that God was reconciling the world to himself in Christ, not counting men's sins against them. And he has committed to us the message of reconciliation."

This would seem to fulfill the second part of the definition for fruit, and it would apply both to individual Christians and to the corporate body of Christ.

The I Am as expressed as the true vine extends through all of human history as branches producing fruit until Revelation 20:11-12a, "Then I saw a great white throne and Him who was seated on it. Earth and sky fled from His presence, and there was no place for them. And I saw the dead, great and small, standing before the throne, and books were opened. Another book was opened, which is the book of life." And finally, Revelation 20:15, states, "If anyone's name was not found written in the book of life, he was thrown into the lake of fire."

We find the final I Am statement in John 18:4-6. "Jesus, knowing all that was going to happen to Him, went out and asked them, 'Who is it you want?'

"'Jesus of Nazareth,' they replied.

"'(Ego Eimi) I am he,' Jesus said. (And Judas the traitor was standing there with them.) When Jesus said, "I am He," they drew back and fell to the ground."

This passage differs somewhat from all the others in that there is no direct object of the verb. To review the unique usage, ego eimi means "I I am." The verb stem, "es," is the root of the verb and we define it as, "be" or "to be." When modified with the suffix, "-mi," that changes the verb, "es," to the first person singular, "eimi," or "I am." In order for this to make sense in English, it translates to, "I Am He." That does not make this final usage of that phrase less significant, if for no other reason than His response causes the detachment of soldiers and some officials from the chief priests and Pharisees being guided by Judas to draw back and fall to the ground. If we take this literally, it would seem to show that there was a physical reaction to Jesus simply uttering the phrase.

Twice John fell down before the angel speaking with him to

worship the angel, in Revelation 19:10 and 22:9, and the angel warned him, "Do not do it! I am your fellow servant." If the presence of an angel can cause such a response in someone, how much more when confronted by the I Am. John also had such a confrontation with Jesus in Revelation 1:17 where he wrote, "When I saw Him, I fell at His feet as though dead. Then He placed His right hand on me and said: 'Do not be afraid. I am the First and the Last.'" In the garden of Gethsemane Jesus was no less the "First and the Last" but He did not yet have the same appearance as with John's encounter in the Revelation.

*Lord, we thank You for the time we have spent in Your Word. Touch our hearts and minds with the things we have studied and allow us to become your agents of change in this fallen world. Thank You for sending Your Son, Jesus. We are grateful for Your sacrifice on the cross so that we may have eternal life. We look forward to either meeting You in the air or joining You in heaven when we die. We give You praise and glory in all things for all that You do in our lives, Amen.*